GW01471484

Crowns and Shillings

The History of the Hastings' May Queen

Barry and Helen Jones

This book is dedicated to the memory of Miss Dorothy Catt

Also to the Dancers, both past and present,
who bring "Youth, Beauty and Innocence to the day".

Published in Hastings, Great Britain in 2015
by Barry Jones,
83 Burry Road, St Leonards TN37 6QY
Text copyright © Barry Jones

Printed by Hastings Printing Company Limited

The Author asserts his moral right to be identified as the author of this work
All photographs remain the copyright of the individual contributors.
A catalogue record for this book is available from the British Library

978-0-9933057-0-2

❧ Contents ❧

A brief history of May Day and the Maypole 7

A brief history of the May Queen 10

The origins of the Hastings May Queen 14

Miss Catt and the Orchard School 16

The history of the May Queens of Hastings

May Queens   1934 – 1950 18

                    1951 - 1969 52

                    1970 - 1990 83

                    1991 – 2015 104

Organisers and Dance Directors 147

Hastings May Queens Role of Honour 148

Bibliography 150

Acknowledgements 151

❧ Prologue ❧

It is a fact that, initially, the modern May Queen Pageant was a contrived event. I would maintain that most, if not all, traditional events are contrived, or ultimately evolved in a contrived manner. In Hastings, the Jack-in-the-Green and Bonfire events are prime examples. But the reason for the conception, by Ruskin, of the May Queen Pageant was "to celebrate Youth, Beauty and Innocence" and as an escape from the industrialism of the time. The Industrial Revolution was a tremendous life change for the people, and he felt that there was a need to cling onto their roots and traditions. I for one would say that these are two good reasons which would still apply today!

The Hastings May Queen Pageant owes its existence to Miss Dorothy Catt, and Mr J Norman Gray. In its early years it became one of the biggest events of the Hastings Town calendar, but is now seen as a minor part of the Jack-in-the-Green weekend, and could easily be lost forever. However, if we understand the background and the concept perhaps the tradition will be sustained. Some of the photographs in this book may be of poor quality, but it is important that the memories of the event are retained.

Helen and I, as the organisers, have tried to maintain the basic form of Crowning, Pageantry and Dance, but as a less formal and technically minded event. Even so, to watch these young people perform their dance, and the tension of knowing that the ribbons could very easily get plaited the wrong way is a mixture of pleasure and strain we endure each year. The Sunday afternoon gives pleasure to many and we are proud to be associated with it. More importantly, the young people involved are enthusiastic about it and it is wonderful to experience the purity and joy of youth without the cynicism with which the young are usually associated.

Barry Jones
May 2015

🦋 May Day and The Maypole – a brief history 🦋

When humans progressed from wandering hunters to farmers, the seasons of the year became vital components to their lives. The change from the cold barren winter into warmer days, when life returned to the world, was particularly welcomed. It's hard for the modern generations to imagine just how their ancestors' lives were governed by the weather, and how this seasonal transition was paramount to their very existence.

The beginning of May became noted as the time when this transformation occurred, and signs like the opening of the May blossom were taken as symbols of the changes taking place. Subsequently, the people believed that they had to assist these changes and began to devise formal ceremonies.

These various customs became the start of an unbroken tradition of celebrating May Day which still exists today.

As the tree played a large part of their everyday life, in the form of wood for the fire, building and the protection it gave their villages, it's not surprising that gods were attributed to this potent force, and the celebrations were directed at these entities.

In time, there were reports of tall trees being cut down, stripped of all but the top growth, and brought back to the village. These were then erected near the village and the young would dance around this most powerful symbol to show thanks for the warmer days and the promise of fertility.

An Elizabethan woodcut of Maypole, dancers and musicians

There are various reasons suggested for the use of a pole, including as a representation of the Tree of Life on which Christ was sacrificed to cleanse the world, or the hub of the wheel of the Heavens around which the people danced to bring order and shape back to the world. Of course, the phallic nature of the pole cannot be overlooked. In later cultures, their own myths and legends were used to explain the reasoning behind the pole, but the simplicity of erecting such an awe inspiring structure made the tree an obvious choice to be the centre of any festivities.

The earliest representation of a Maypole in England is in drawings of a window at Betley Hall in Staffordshire, built in the mid 1460's during the reign of Edward IV, but later demolished.

 May Day celebrations continued for centuries, taking different forms around the country. There are several accounts of 100ft tall trees being used, although this is probably an exaggeration. Certainly 60 to 80ft would be common. The most famous of these was the Maypole erected off Leadenhall Street in London. It was set up opposite St Andrews Church, which is now known as St Andrews Undershaft. This Maypole was erected every May until student riots in 1517 caused it to be brought down. Although reinstated, the pole of 1547 was seized by a mob that destroyed it because it was seen as a pagan symbol.

These festivities came to an abrupt halt when Oliver Cromwell outlawed all forms of dance and festivities. Even then, Maypoles were used in some areas as a form of defiance to this Puritanical rule.

The Restoration of the Monarchy (1661) allowed the celebrations to continue, and indeed flourish. A law was created to order that Maypoles were erected and the Morris was danced! Local areas added to, and updated their traditions and the celebrations started to become more formal.

Gradually, the trees were reduced in size and decorations added. These were usually in the form of foliage and flowers wound round the length, or as a "crown" around the top. Gradually the trees became poles. Sometime in the fifteenth or sixteenth centuries the poles began to be painted. In act 3, scene 2 of "A Midsummer Night's Dream", Shakespeare refers to a painted May Pole. Eventually ribbons were fixed to the top and were used in the dance, and the Maypole became close to what we would recognise today. Although originally a Southern European custom, the ribbons became a more common addition to our Maypoles. The earliest sign of a beribboned maypole in England is in a painting from 1751, although this is rare, but by the middle of the 19th century it became the norm.

Medieval music would have been in the form of pipes and tambours with, occasionally, English bagpipes. From the mid nineteenth century the most popular instruments would be the fiddle and accordion.

It is not known when the dances became formalised. Morris dancing can be dated back to the 1400's, but it is likely that the dances around the pole were less structured until the following century. Mostly consisting of a "chain" dance, where the dancers join hands and skip and dance around the tree, the dancing was just a show of joy and celebration for all the folk of the village. As the celebrations became more formal and part of a pageant or showpiece, dances were created to be performed for the benefit of an audience. Then, as the ribbons were added and the potential of a variety of shapes was realised, the dancing slowly evolved into the form we know today.

❧ Later years – Resurgence and Threats ❧

The frolics of May Day have been well documented over the last 800 years, as has been the decline. For some reason the celebrations became muted during the last years of the eighteenth century. It may well be that the industrial revolution took its toll, and the need of the employers to keep the mills and factories working meant that there were no holidays to celebrate. Although the Bank of England closed on four Mondays each year it did not recognise May Day. The 1871 law recognised Easter Monday, Whit Monday, the first Monday in August and Boxing Day. The May Bank Holiday, as we know it today, did not come about until 1978. Throughout this time, however, it must be said that Chimney Sweeps maintained the tradition as they had very little, if any, work to do at that time of year, but even these celebrations began to die out in the late nineteenth century. A resurgence of interest in National Traditions began in the 1970's, leading to the reinstatement of numerous pageants and celebrations around the country. Regretfully, there are a number of these which have either been stopped or are in danger due to the cost of insurance or health and safety issues.

❧ The May Queen – a brief history ❧

By the late Middle Ages the May Day celebrations were well established and participants were starting to have roles to play. In some parts of Europe there are accounts of May King races in which the winner held office for a year. Because of the prestige of these races the outcome was very often violent and emotions ran high. In England, the ribald celebrations continued for centuries and only became curtailed through Puritan legislation and morals. There are many examples of letters from the clergy through the post Norman invasion years which demand that the revelries be stopped.

The major character of the late medieval age was Robin Hood, and in the Churchwardens and Chamberlain's book of Kingston-upon-Thames of 1480, was an entry for "Robin Hood and May Games". This included "For paynting of a banner for Robin Hood... £0-0s-3d" The May Games were traditionally held at Pentecost and although this means that the date can vary, usually the earliest date is around the 10th May. This would lend some credence to the ides that "May Day" was originally celebrated on the 12th. (See 1943).

Under Henry VIII, one of the entries in 1522 was "To Mayde Marian, for her labours for two years …. £0 2s 0d. The same phrase and monetary unit used in the modern day Hastings Pageants. (One shilling per annum, albeit in the form of a brooch). The Robin Hood character was seen as the main cause of celebration of the time, and from the lowest status to the highest, men would dress in the green costume of that character. In 1603 an historian, Stow, wrote in his "A survey of London" that "King Henry and his wife, Katherine, with their courtiers" rode out Maying dressed as Robin Hood.

In 1547, Bishop Latimer in a sermon preached in front of Edward VI uses the phrase "Robin Hode's Day" to refer to May Day, and in 1613 a "Lord of the May" makes an appearance in a comic play.

However the Maid Marion character first appeared in a French play in 1280. At this time she was not connected to Robin, but was introduced into the May games around 1475, and it must have seemed an obvious development to create a love interest between the two. Within a few years Marion had become recognised as the partner to Robin Hood and a new legend was created. In these games, Robin was seen to be the" King of May" or the "Summer King", and it is logical to assume that Marion would be his "Queen". This arrangement persisted for many years, going into the 17th Century but Marion eventually became associated with the Morris, and took the form of Malkin, a character who transformed into a slovenly Hag-type woman.

Eventually the emphasis settled on the female element. Girls were dressed in white with floral decorations in their hair, and were taken around the village with garlands to spread good luck and fertility. Garlands have consistently figured in accounts of the celebrations, and in some form or another, have been ever-present in celebrating May Day although, sadly, the custom is now close to dying out altogether. In Sussex, the 1st of May was known as Garland Day up until the 1920's. Strangely, garland making was restricted to the South, West and Midlands of England, and rarely reached beyond those areas. The old children's' rhyme "Here we go gathering nuts in May" is a derivation of" knots of May" meaning garlands, and in Lewes a "Garland day" is held each May bank holiday to celebrate this. The organisers are a women's Morris side called Knots of May.

Some cultures celebrating May Day used a version of a female legend or Goddess as a symbol of the day. The most well-known suggestion for the prototype May Queen is the Roman goddess Flora, although Keith Leech in his book, "The Hastings Traditional Jack-in-the-Green", shows this is inaccurate due to the variance of dates. Many other earth figures appear to be possible models for the May Queen, and there is even a connection with the Virgin Mary. Maia, the mother of Mercury is another, but she was portrayed by a grotesque figure as "The May Lady". However, as the myths of the Maypole show, the explanations may well be cultural interpretations of what is a centuries old evolved custom.

In the 1731 paper, Waldron's "Description of the Isle of Man" there is an account of a Queen of May and Queen of Winter ceremony, in which the two lead their armies in a fight for supremacy. Obviously the outcome is pre-determined and the summer is reclaimed. A similar ritual takes place in parts of Scandinavia, which suggests it derives from the Viking age. At this time there are very few traditions which name a "May Queen" as the central figure.

Going into the 19th Century, the celebrations continued with subtle variations around the country and although there were" May Queens", they were often accompanied by a young man and were known as the Lord and Lady of May.

John Collier's "Queen Guinevre's Maying"

In the above picture, painted in 1900, you can see the characters of Robin and Marion, both in the foreground and, not so clear, the riders behind.

In 1881 John Ruskin, the noted philosopher and critic, approached Whitelands College in London with a new concept. Ruskin had a true Romantics view of a May Queen in line with his religious beliefs and as a reaction to the industrialism of the times. He felt that industrialisation had robbed each worker of their individuality, and of the beauty in the world. His belief was that May Day should be a joyous celebration of "Youth, Beauty and Innocence". Therefore it was his suggestion to the Head of college, John Faunthorpe, that a May Queen of the type we know today be created. Between these two men the new Pageant was worked through and Whitelands College became the birthplace of the modern May Queen. As it was a teaching college, the young ladies spread this form of Pageant to the outside world very quickly, and within twenty years the Crowning of the May Queen became established as a countrywide tradition amongst schools and small institutions. In most cases (like Hastings) it was a local teacher of Dance, Drama, Speech or even Acrobatics who introduced the tradition as a Town or Village wide affair.

Very few villages or towns have an unbroken record of May Festivals in the modern era. Knutsford in Cheshire can date theirs back to 1864 and is probably the oldest existing tradition of its kind in the Country. Their Pageant evolved into the Whitelands style in the 1890s.Virtually all of the rest are less than 100 years old and most are less than 60. So the Hastings Pageant, at 80 years plus, is a noteworthy event and more special than most people realise.

Nowadays you can find May Queen ceremonies around the world. America, Australia, Guyana and Qatar are some of the many countries to where our English custom has been exported. Some parts of Canada boast May Day celebrations going back to the late 19th century.

The village of Stanion, Northamptonshire was the home of the first non-white May Queen. In 1923 the pupils of the village school cast their votes and one of two daughters of an African seaman was elected.

Ruskin decreed that a May Queen should be chosen "as the Likeablest and Loveablest of her peers", and that the May Day Pageant "should celebrate Youth, Beauty and Innocence". We hope that you will agree.

The first report of a May Queen in Hastings is in the May 1911 "Hastings Pictorial" and was created by the Holy Trinity Girls Club. Note the Jack-in-the-Green. In Hastings, at least, the Jack was a May time symbol that would figure in a lot of the subsequent May Queen celebrations

Nowadays there is a perception of the Jack-in-the-Green that it has mythological or pagan origins, but all research shows that it is merely an evolved garland. The chimney sweeps of Hastings were enthusiastic May revellers and would parade a Jack around the town each May Day. In the late nineteenth century the custom began to die out, and the sightings of a Jack were few and far between. Consequently it is of historical interest to see children invoking this tradition to celebrate May Day in this decade. The fact that this entertainment was arranged by the Holy Trinity Church, and that this Jack was carried by a girl (Mabel White), is an indication of the acceptance of this tradition by a Christian society who would recognise this form of May celebration.

Because of the Whitelands origins, schools seem to be the driving force behind the introduction of the new May Pageants and several schools in Hastings were soon to adopt this "tradition". In Westfield the school log shows that, in 1913, the children were allowed out of school early in order to prepare for the May Queen celebrations and Daisy Ray was crowned in front of pupils, friends and parents. However, the May Day celebrations suffered after 1916 due to the introduction of Empire Day as an annual event each 24th May. The energy of the schools was directed to this, and for several years May Queen celebrations were in danger of disappearing from Hastings altogether. Ten years later two things were initiated which would be significant for the tradition...

In April 1926, the Foundation stone was laid for the new White Rock Theatre In the May of 1926 Miss Dorothy Catt opened the Orchard School of Speech and Drama and within a few years the Hastings May Queen Pageant was secure.

Halton School May Queen 1914 (bl)

The Orchard School at Bal Edmund (mc)

❧ Miss Catt and the Orchard School ❧

In 1934, Miss Dorothy Catt, a Speech and Drama school proprietor, asked Hastings Council if she could produce a Pageant of dance and music which would include the Crowning of a Hastings May Queen. The Entertainments Manager of the time, Mr J. Norman Gray responded enthusiastically and agreed to promote the event.

Dorothy Catt was the daughter of a milkman who lived in Burry Road and worked in the Silverhill area of St Leonards-on-sea. Later, they moved to Warrior Square This may have had some connection to the location of the original May Queen Pageant.

 Although the Speech and Drama school was known as "The Orchard School", in 1926 it was just a room above at the Silverhill Club which was used as the local "Palais du Dance". In 1928 the school moved to the premises next door at No 6 Sedlescombe Road South. Around 1937 Miss Catt's school then moved to the building which was originally called Bal Edmund and was located in Upper Church

Road. This building was later demolished and there now stands a block of flats with the same name. In 1946, the school was moved to Radcliffe House at 199 Sedlescombe Road North. This house was to be the realisation of Miss Catt's dream. As a child, living in Burry Road, she used to walk past Radcliffe House on her way to school. She was to recall later, to her pupils, that she dreamt of owning that house one day. Ion Castro, a former pupil, remembers the house with awe, particularly the sweeping driveway with a mass of Pampas grass in the centre. Co-incidentally, this house was built for George Burry Clement, after whom Burry Road was named. Again, regretfully, Radcliffe was demolished and is now a housing development called Radcliffe Close. In both cases the pupils numbered about 50 and would become the life-blood of the May Queen Pageant for the next 16 years.

Miss Catt was to produce the Pageant for the next 40 years.

Although there have been many changes to the ceremony over the years, the characters and features of the first crowning were maintained for a remarkably long time, a testament to Miss Catt's research and planning. She based her pageants on information from many sources, in particular Chamber's Book of Day and Brand's Antiquities. Although the dances were arranged by a variety of different local teachers, the Pageants were under the overall Direction of Miss Catt until the 1970's

Miss Catt's father (foreground, left) with his milk cart (apm)

❧ The History of the May Queens of Hastings ❧

The crowning of Queen Rhona Powell. Our first May Queen (mc)

1934

Queen Rhona Powell

The first pageant was held on Tuesday the first of May 1934. Alderman Henry Burden, the Mayor of Hastings, crowned Rhona Powell on a day of brilliant sunshine in front of a crowd which took the organisers by surprise for its size and enthusiasm. The Chief Constable of Sussex also attended.

The revels opened with the Oxfordshire Children's May Song, a feature of the day that would continue for decades.

"Good Morning Lords and Ladies
It is the First of May
We hope you'll view our Garlands
That are so bright and gay"

During the festivities, the garlands were taken around the crowd. These were covered with a white linen cloth, and were "shown" in exchange for alms. These donations were collected in long handled, flower bedecked nets, and the money given to the Mayor's charity fund.

The dancing started with folk dances;" Meeting six", "Hyde Park", "The Spaniard" and "Flowers of Edinburgh". Next were National dances of Scotland, Wales and Ireland, followed by two Morris Jigs and "Bacca Pipes".

The folk dances and Morris were arranged by Miss Mabel Willis of the English Folk Dance Society, the Nationals by Miss Marjorie V. Kent. Miss Willis also arranged the Maypole dancing which was to follow. After the initial dancing, the star of the show appeared. Rhona Powell was escorted into the arena by the Herald, a group of maids of Honour and a Page. She wore a dress that was designed by Miss G Armitage, a student of the Hastings School of Art, and made by Mastin Bros. a local department store which will be remembered by many local residents. The dress was a white gown ornamented with flowers and leaves, with a graceful train lined with pink.

Gladys Armitage went on to become the Hastings Carnival queen in 1937.

Alderman Burden crowned Rhona with a "Primrose Chaplet" which was composed of primroses and wallflowers. Unfortunately the crown was too small, and several attempts to secure it were unsuccessful. Eventually a crown that was used in rehearsal was located and substituted for the real one, and the ceremony was completed

The Queen sat on her throne for the ceremony, which was a carved chair that had been in Miss Catt's family for over 100 years. It was personally decorated with flowers and foliage by Mr G Haig, the Superintendent of the Parks and Gardens.

Queen Rhona with Alderman Burden (ho)

A photograph of Henry Burden can be seen in the Nationwide Building Society premises in Hastings as a member of the Hastings Permanent Building Society Board of Directors of December 1926.

A cry went up from the character of Robin Hood: "We hail thee, Queen of May" as the Queen was presented with a flower tipped sceptre. Miss Catt had obviously noted the importance of Robin Hood as a May Day symbol, and decided to respect the historical tradition.

Robin Hood presents the Sceptre *(mc)*

The afternoon culminated with the Maypole dances, "Barbers' Pole", "Single Plait", "Double Plait", "Gypsies Tent" and ""Spiders' Web".

The pupils of Miss Catt's "Orchard School of Speech and Drama" made up the bulk of the entertainment, and it was this school which supplied the May Queens and characters for many years to come, although the honour was alternated with Miss Phyllis Godfrey's dance school from 1950 onwards.

It was such a special day that Miss Catt was to write later that "The mayor was so excited that it looked as if, at any moment, he would break into a Morris Jig"
The event was deemed to be significant enough to be filmed by a Pathe news team and shown in cinemas nationwide.

Showing the Garlands (ho)

The first Maypole dancing at Warrior Square (ho)

Folk dancing (ho)

Although the Pageant was reported at the time to follow "age old traditions" it was obviously an amalgam of the Whitelands ceremony and the characters of the celebrations of the previous century. The girls were dressed in early19th Century costume and the theme of the event was "Merrie England" .This is emphasised by the use of a major character to be used in future pageants," The Prince of Merrie England" This role was often played by the outgoing May Queen and held some importance.

This representation of old England as seen through rose tinted glasses is often ridiculed in today's society, but is surely just an echo of John Ruskin's vision of celebrating youth, innocence and beauty.

Part of the Warrior Square audience 1934 (ho)

1935

Queen Margaret Hewett

After the success of this first Pageant, Hastings council allowed Dorothy Catt to make it an annual event, and even produced a printed programme.

In 1935 the Mayoress, Mrs Lancelot Blackman, crowned Margaret Hewett (13) as the new May Queen. This was to be the first time the event took place in Alexandra Park, at what's called the Lower Lawn (the large lawn inside the main Park Gates). After the singing of the May Song, 3 English dances and a Morris Jig there followed 8 Swedish folk dances and two 17th Century Morris dances. Then the sight of the May Queen elect brought into the Park on a "Flower Decked chariot" to the sound of a bugle. She made her entrance into the Park through what was described as the "Spa Gates". These gates were situated opposite the bottom of St Helens Park Road, where, today, there is a smaller entrance. After the crowning, the same Maypole dances followed but with the addition of "Amos Amat", whilst the Queen "toured" around and amongst the crowd.

Queen Margaret tours the Lawn (ho)

Mrs Blackman crowns Queen Margaret (ho)

The dances were under the direction of Miss Mabel Willis. Young Margaret Hewett was the daughter of a local wine merchant and a pupil of Miss Catt's speech and drama school. Consequently she was well educated and well spoken. This latter was put to the test when it was revealed that she was to appear on the BBC. After the crowning, she was taken, along with her retinue to London and made an appearance on the popular evening radio show "In Town Tonight". The broadcast started with the singing of the Oxfordshire May Song and, after an interview with the May Queen, ended with The Maypole song. Peter Duncan, the producer of the show, may have been an old friend of Miss Catt's, or even a past pupil.

COUNTY BOROUGH OF HASTINGS.
Entertainments Manager   J. NORMAN GRAY.

THE CROWNING
OF THE
QUEEN OF MAY

BY
PUPILS OF THE
ORCHARD SCHOOL
ST. LEONARDS-ON-SEA,
ON
MAY DAY, 1935,
IN
THE ALEXANDRA PARK.
At 3 p.m.

The Ceremony arranged by   Dances under the direction of
Miss DOROTHY CATT.   Miss MABEL WILLIS,
                                   F.I.R.A.P.T., M.R.S.T., M.E.F.D.S.
Music directed by Mrs. E. M. GRIFFITHS.
Piano - Miss BETTY FIELDING.   'Cello - Miss G. PITMAN.

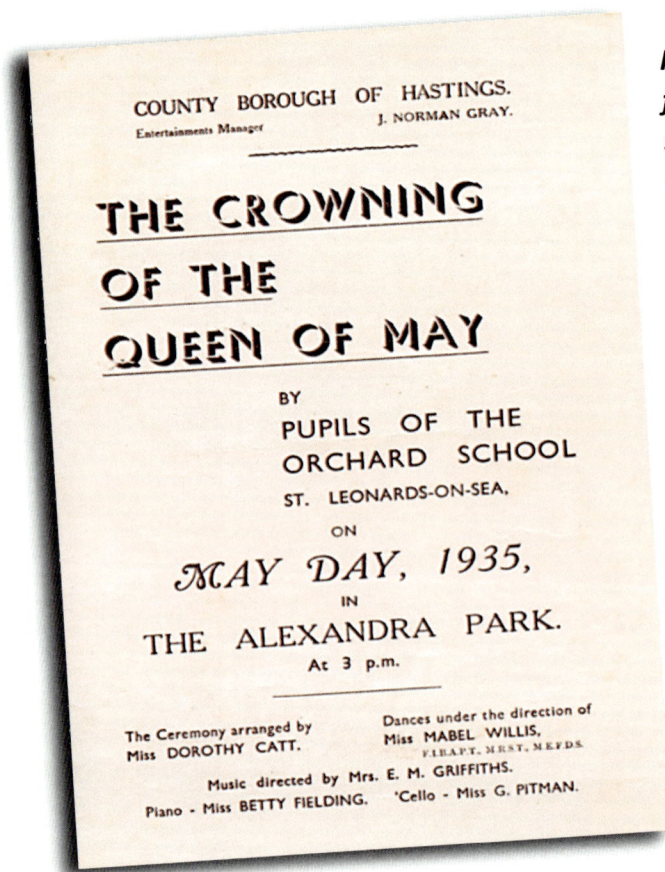

Programmes were sold for one shilling or sixpence (1/- or 6d) dependant on where you sat.

1936

Queen Peggy Ashman

This time the May Queen arrived at the Main Park Gates in a "flower bedecked chariot" and was crowned by another Mayoress, Mrs EH Ford. This year also saw the appearance, for the first time, of a Chimney Sweep. It had been recorded in the Daily Graphic magazine that Miss Catt had "endeavoured to make the celebration as true to old time tradition as possible", and "is making all effort to procure a friendly chimney sweep who will participate in the revelry" This was a Mr William S. Knight, who became a regular feature of the event. It is interesting to note that, in the modern times, the Sweep is described as "lucky", but in the 1936 programme he is just "A Chimney Sweep". Miss Catt's research had shown an intimate connection to the sweeps with May Day and she had invited Mr Knight as a traditional May Day feature and not as a lucky charm.

In furtherance of the traditions of the past, he brought with him a Jack-in-the-Green (Mr H. Edwards) This was a connection to the old May Day custom of Chimney Sweeps who "went out" each May 1st to celebrate the day and whose garlands got bigger each year to compete with other Sweeps' families offerings, until the garland was as big as the man (jack). Eventually, the garland was carried from inside (Jack-in-the-Green) and grew even taller. Today's Hastings Jack is an evolution of the original, whereas the Jones family carry a forerunner of the Jack, a large garland which has yet to evolve into the classic "Jack" shape.

Mr Knight was to accompany the May Queen for the next 32 years.

Other attendants were, as before, Maids of Honour, Pages, Herald and Robin Hood.

Mrs Ford crowns Queen Peggy (ho)

An impressive programme included five National dances, seven folk dances and six Maypole dances. The Nationals were arranged by Miss Joyce Tidman M.R.A.D. (Inter Cert), and the Folk were taught by Miss M Coombes E.F.D.S.

1936 was the year that the May Queen was presented the Shilling "for her labours" for the first time. In an additional ceremony, after leaving the Park, Queen Peggy was taken to the White Rock Pavilion to be presented with the shilling by the Entertainments Manager, Mr J Norman Gray. This gift was to become established as a regular feature in future Pageants, and for a few years it was customary for this to take place at the White Rock. Eventually the presentation of the Shilling was to be part of the crowning ceremony. As seen previously, the records from 1522 have shown a two shilling payment to Maid Marion for "her labours for two years, and Miss Catt had reinstated the tradition but on a yearly basis. Another reminder of just how assiduous she had been in her research.

An additional feature this year was the gala event in Alexandra Park in July. Entitled "At the Court of The May Queen", it was another showpiece for Miss Catt's school and the dancing arranged by the Misses Tidman and Coombe

Queen Peggy arrives through the Park Gates (ho)

Regretfully, no pictures of the "chariot" survive. The above shows Queen Peggy, having descended, processing from the main Park Gates.

Peggy was chosen by a ballot of the pupils of the Orchard School, and the result was announced by J Norman Grey, continuing the strong support from the Council for this event.

Peggy lived, with her parents, at Palace Chambers and was a keen swimmer. She had competed in several London championships, and her ambition was to compete in the 1940 Olympic Games. An ambition, sadly, that was never going to be fulfilled as the war would prevent the Olympics from taking place.

Madaleen Aukett was a close runner up in the election.

A rare shot of Mr J Norman Gray as he announces the result of the ballot (mc)

Rehearsals were held in the wooded part of the upper Park (mc)

Peggy is pictured on one of the old Park bridges (mc)

: : Programme : :

1. **The Oxfordshire Childrens' May Song**

   "Good morning, Lords and Ladies
   It is the First of May,
   We hope you'll view our garlands
   They are so sweet and gay."

   To maintain the traditional element, "certain children will go through the May Day custom of collecting alms" in return for showing their garlands.

2. **National Dances**

1.	Hornpipe	Jacqueline Ashman
2.	Sword Dance	Barbara Parrish
3.	Fling	Jacqueline Ashman
4.	Irish Jig	Madaleen Aukett
5.	Welsh Dance	Betty Tingle

   Folk Dances

1.	Long Eight	Junior Group
2.	Geud Man of Ballangeugh	Senior Group
3.	The First of April	Junior Group
4.	Hunsdon House	Senior Group
5.	Goddesses	Junior Group
6.	Epping Forest	Senior Group
7.	Durham Reel	Ensemble

May Song	Traditional

ARRIVAL OF MAY QUEEN IN HER FLOWER DECKED CHARIOT
accompanied by her train.

The Crowning of the Queen by
THE MAYORESS OF HASTINGS
(Mrs. E. M. Ford)

Triumphal March Past.

"The after part of the day is chiefly spent in dancing round a tall Poll, which is called a May Poll. . . ."

The Maypole Dance

1. The Barber's Pole
2. The Single Plait
3. The Double Plait
4. The Gipsy's Tent
5. The Spider's Web
6. The Ropes

FINALE.

Queen of the May	Peggy Ashman
Maids of Honour	Margaret Griffiths, Irene Mitchell
	Sheila Coleman, Pauline Hilder
	Shirley Cruttenden, Connie Clark
Pages	Billy Worsley, Terry Fairey
	Patrick Wick
Herald	May Baker
Robin Hood	Maureen Cooper
Senior Dancing Group	Betty Ashman, Dorothy Taylor,
	Olive Taylor, Betty Tingle,
	Doris Ventris, Madaleen Aukett,
	Barbara Parrish, Peggy Nye
Junior Dancing Group	Pauline Porter, Pamela Taylor,
	Margaret Sulter, Betsy Goldie-
	Taubman, Jacqueline Ashman,
	Joan Huxford, June Parker,
	Peggy Bedwell, Eileen Fogerty
Master of the Ceremonies	
Jack-in-the-Green	
A Chimney Sweep	

Inside the 1936 Programme

1937

Queen May Baker

Queen May with Mayoress Mrs. Doreen Blackman (ho)

Another ceremony at Alexandra Park saw 14 year old May Baker crowned by the Mayoress, Mrs Doreen Blackman (previously named as Mrs Lancelot Blackman as it was common practise to refer to the wife in her husband's name). May was chosen by a ballot at the Orchard school, and was described as a tall, fair-haired Irish girl who loved horses. The voting was close, and she only just pipped Betty Tingle to the post.

The dancing was arranged by Miss Dorothy Purrott, and would have been quite impressive as there were 6 Maypole dances, 9 National and 12 English folk dances, with a finale of the Sailor's Hornpipe by Jacqueline Ashman and the corps de ballet. The last was Nicholas Elton dancing "John Bull".

Mr Knight with one of the flower girls *(mc)*

Mr Knight appears to have perched the young lady on the brush, which would suggest that, like the modern sweeps, he kept a clean brush especially for "ceremonial purposes".

1938

Queen Peggy Nye

Mrs Blackman, the Mayoress, crowned Peggy Nye in Alexandra Park after the Pageant had been postponed twice due to bad weather. To prove that May Day washouts are not just a recent phenomenon, 1938 had its share of heavy rain and bitingly cold wind. Rather than switch to an indoor venue, it was decided to return to the Park at a later date.

Watching Queen Peggy being crowned are the Sweep and the Jack-in-the-Green (ho)

After two postponements, Peggy was crowned in front of a crowd of just a few dozen people. The weather was still very cold and windy. The Deputy Mayor, Councillor Dr W.E. Jameson, greeted the May Queen and made a speech after the crowning. He was the Chairman of the Hastings and St Leonards District Nursing Association who were the beneficiaries of the Alms collection. National and English folk dancing and a Tarantelle concluded the ceremony, which again was organised by Miss Catt and Miss Dorothy Purrot . Mr Knight the sweep brought along his son who appeared as a Jack-in-the-Green.

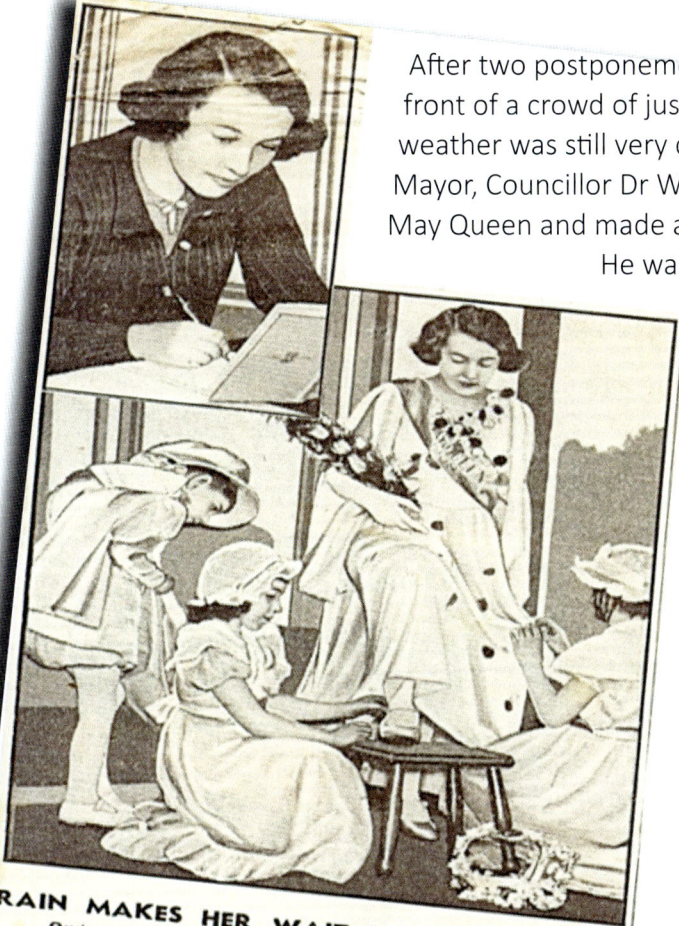

RAIN MAKES HER WAIT FOR HER CROWN

Owing to rain, 13-years-old Peggy Nye has to wait for her crown as Hastings May Queen. She was dressed in her coronation robes when she was told that the ceremony had been postponed. So Peggy (above) went back to her studies,

(ho)

1939

Queen Molly Parsons

The ill health of Miss Catt meant that a grand Pageant could not be arranged this year. Consequently the Crowning became a private affair, held in the grounds of the original home of the Orchard School of Speech and Drama, Bal Edmund.   From her bedroom window Miss Catt could look down on to the ceremony and a hastily erected Maypole.

Unfortunately, she had suffered a bad fall which had damaged both knees. This was to cause long term problems and the onset of arthritis. We do not know quite how badly she suffered with her knees, but it would mean that she would become more dependent on other dance teachers and their schools. Miss Purrott again directed the dance.

Queen Molly has the distinction of being the youngest Hastings May Queen. Aged just 10, she was crowned by the Mayoress, Mrs E M Ford.

Another point of note is that Bal Edmund was one of the many local houses worked on by Robert Tressel. Although not in the book "The Ragged Trousered Philanthropist", it is known that the author was familiar with Bal Edmund, and had worked here a few times.

Queen Molly with her twin sister Dorothy (mc)

Mrs Ford crowns Molly (mc)

Queen Molly and entourage (mc)

1940

Queen Norma Excell

The war had changed the daily life of the Country, and it was to the credit of the Town that events like the Crowning of the May Queen were taking place. A large public display was out of the question so another venue was found. The garden of the vicarage of St John's church which was adjacent to Bal Edmund was used for the crowning of Norma Excell. The Mayoress, Mrs E M Ford officiated, and her son, Sub Lieutenant John Ford RN, also attended.

Another wartime feature was the presence of London evacuees, and pupils from Hughes Field and Old Woolwich Road Schools in Greenwich participated. So, strangely, both the Hastings and the Greenwich May Queens were crowned in the same place at the same time. Mrs Ford crowned both Norma Excell of Hastings and Lucy Eccott the May Queen of Greenwich.

There followed "the Dances of the Allies", which was a collection of dances, in the national costumes of Britain, Scandinavia and France. The director of dance, this year, was Miss Kathleen Neal.

The event was produced by Miss Catt and Miss Taylor of Greenwich, and their pupils were seen to dance around two Maypoles at the same time, which must have been quite a sight.

Unfortunately, the weather was "disappointing" in that it was cold and overcast.

The two May Queens (Norma seated) (mc)

The Maypoles of Hastings and Greenwich (mc)

1941

Queen Gwen Watford

Our most famous May Queen so far. Queen Gwen went on to become an actress of some repute. Appearing in a couple of films in the late fifties, she became a household name through the sixties for her TV work. Gwen was trained in speech and drama by Miss Catt.

At the age of 14, however, she was being crowned as the Hastings May Queen at St John's Vicarage in St Leonards This was a small affair, with only two or three dances arranged by Miss Neal. As a special treat, and as compensation for a lack of pomp, she was taken around Silverhill on the back of a gun carriage. This is an indicator of the nature of the defences in Hastings at the time. The fact that it was a simple task to get hold of a gun carriage tells us that Hastings was well stocked in that direction.

Gwen was mentioned in the autobiography "Sir John Gielgud, a life in letters". A wealthy lady named Gertrude Jefferson persuaded Sir John to visit Hastings to see Gwen in a school performance whilst he was casting for a young actress to play Teresa in the play "The Cradle Song". In a letter to Dorothy Catt dated 18th November 1943 he wrote that, "Although she was undoubtedly talented", he felt she should continue her schooling, but that when she had done so, he would introduce her to a leading Dramatic School. He went on to help her get her first acting job, and continued to take a great interest in her long and distinguished career

Unfortunately, the war had another impact on the event. The Council was not able to present the Queen with her "shilling". This shortfall was made up for at a later date, but she had to wait until 1960 before she received it at a special ceremony during the May Queen Pageant of that year. Regretfully, there appear to be no photographs of this year's event available.

Forty years later, Gwen was to present the Hastings Music Festival with the Dorothy Catt memorial cup for drama.

1942

Queen Elizabeth Hayward

St John's vicarage again was the venue for the ceremony as the Mayor, Councillor Rymill, crowned Elizabeth Hayward. The weather had been cold and wet, and so it was on May Day. The ceremony was made even shorter than it had been intended and, although it was perfunctory, we must thank Miss Catt for maintaining the unbroken record of the Pageant.

1943

Queen Lavender Seaward

Although the war was reaching a turning point in Europe, the dangers still existed on the home front. Consequently St John's was again the chosen venue. Lavender was crowned by Alderman Hussey who was, at that point, Deputy Mayor. The ceremony though, was beginning to resemble the Pageants of previous years with National dances resuming under the direction of Miss Kathleen Neal. The event was made bigger by the inclusion of the Crowning of the Sedlescombe May Queen, Rowena Gammon, and by having two Maypoles and two sets of Maypole dancers. Sedlescombe was to have its own "Queens Court on the village green in due course.

As her family were known to have lived at Lavender Cottage, it is probable that the May Queen was named after her place of birth.

As an example of Miss Catt's research, this year's Pageant was held at a later date. Because of the bad weather of the last two or three years, she decided to hold the event later in the month. She had determined that, according to the old calendar, May Day falls on the Wednesday nearest to the 12th of the month, and this year the 12th was a Wednesday. So, consequently, that's when this Pageant took place. The medieval May Games were held at Pentecost which, although variable, usually starts around the 10th May. The Gregorian calendar took over from the Julian in order to correct the imperfections which meant that, from September 1752, the UK "lost" 11 days. Miss Catt had assumed that this meant the original celebrations had taken place on the twelfth, but there is scant evidence to support this.

Another interesting fact arising from this change is that Lady Day (25th March) was traditionally the date when rents were due. After the change of calendar, this date was amended to the 6th April which, to this day, is the date of the start of the UK tax year.

1944

Queen Mavis Stapley

For the last time, St John's was chosen as the venue for a Pageant, and Queen Mavis was crowned by Councillor Mrs A.W. Farnfield (a name to remember for later), who was deputising for Alderman Hussey

Pupils of Glenthorne and Bal Edmund schools danced the National dances and a "Galopede" under the direction of Miss Neal. A Galopede is a quick dance in 2/4 time. With a piano and violin for the music, everything seemed to be getting back to normal. Garlands for pennies were shown, which suggests the audience was increasing in size.

At St John's Vicarage for the crowning of Queen Mavis (ho)

1945

Queen Joan Parks

As the wartime danger passed, the Pageant returned to a more prominent venue, Warrior Square. There was a more festive air about the event, and after the May Song and National dances, May Moulton played popular tunes on the banjo.

Joan Parks (14) of 49, Alma Villas, was crowned by the Mayoress, Mrs. Lancelot Blackman, but the shilling presentation again was performed as a separate action. This time it was presented Mr E.W. Clements, a local businessman, at the White Rock. Mr Knight the Chimney Sweep was there, as usual, as were the "garlands for pennies "and the Jack-in-the-Green. As Joan entered the arena her train was held by three children, all under three years of age. The afternoon finished with a ballet display. Again, all the dances were arranged by Miss Kathleen Neal. Miss Catt as usual produced the whole thing.

Queen Joan processes around Warrior Square (ho)

1946

Queen Hazel Jones

Now apparently re-established back at its birthplace of Warrior Square, the Pageant had regained the prestige of former years. An audience of 4000 watched as the Mayor, Councillor F.W. Chambers crowned 14 year old Hazel Jones. As usual the Oxfordshire May song started the celebrations, followed by the National dances. One addition this year was a series of Minstrel plays. The May Queen, from Loose Farm Telham was escorted into the arena by the Chairman of the Entertainments Committee, Councillor P.T. Morrow. In his address to the May Queen, the Mayor asked her to order her subjects (the young people of Hastings) to care for the flora and fauna of the town, and to respect the environment. The Queen concurred in her speech, and another new "tradition" was born. This became a regular addition to the May Queen speech in forthcoming events.

Another "tradition" was started this year. For the first time the dancing was under the direction of Miss Phyllis Godfrey, whose involvement with the May Queen was to last for the next twenty years.

A fine overall view of the 1946 Pageant (mc)

Queen Hazel and entourage (ho)

*Miss Phyliss Godfrey in her
dancing days (pa)*

1947

Queen Claudine Burton

Now the Deputy Mayor, Councillor Mrs A.W.Farnfield attended the Pageant which again took place in Warrior Square Gardens. Queen Claudine (11) of 4 Western Road was one of the youngest May Queens in Hastings.

Along with the ever present Chimney Sweep, the event was attended by the Town Clerk, Mr N.P. Lester.

Pupils of Glenthorne Dance School performed, and this year were joined by jesters and tumblers from Bexhill Amateur Athletic Club.

To indicate the strength of support from Hastings Council, Councillor Rymill was credited as Stage Manager.

The dances were arranged by Phyllis Godfrey and the whole event produced by Miss Catt.

To assist with the collection from the Garlands for Pennies, the Chimney Sweep, Mr W.S. Knight "volunteered" to kiss any lady for a donation. It is not known how successful he was, but the total sum collected on the day reached £5.00. This was given to the Lord Mayor of London's flood disaster fun. March 1947 was the time of the worst floods of the Thames Valley area in the 20th Century.

Queen Claudine is escorted into the arena by the new Deputy Mayor,
Councillor Mrs Farnfield (ho)

1948

Queen Ann Hills

14 year old Ann Hills was crowned at Linton Gardens. An apparently surprising change to the traditional venue can be explained by the fact that Linton Gardens had just been opened as an "Outdoor Theatre" and the May Queen Pageant was the very first event to take place there. Councillor Mrs Farnfield was again on hand as Deputy Mayor with the Town Clerk, Mr N P Lester, to escort Ann into the natural amphitheatre. Alderman F W Chambers, as Mayor, performed the Crowning. All the Dignitaries wore their full robes of office and were accompanied by the Mace Bearer.

Alderman chambers crowns Queen Ann (ho)

In an extraordinary day of surprises, the first one was the choice of entertainment. The music for the Maypole dance was supplied by Juan and the Sun Lounge Players. The compere was Councillor Rymill and, after being crowned, Queen Ann was escorted around the arena by Councillor H.C. Burgess the Chairman of the Entertainments Committee. Also attending was Councillor Mrs Boyd Alexander, Chairwoman of Parks and Gardens. The May Queen attendants comprised 16 Maids of Honour and 12 pages (all less than 5 years of age). The dancers were from Miss Godfrey's school, and a gymnastic display was given by the Bexhill Amateur Athletics Club.

 This amazing pomp was watched by over 2000 people. Once the Queen had been crowned and the dancing was under way, the reason for the attendance of this range of dignitaries was revealed. The Queen and Mr Knight, the Chimney Sweep, were taken by car to the airfield at Pebsham. They were shown to an airplane on a take-off strip lined by the local ATC. The 'plane was owned by the Hastings and East Sussex Air Services, and a 20 minute flight took them to Croydon airfield, from where they were driven to London in time to be interviewed for the BBC In Town Tonight programme. In the interview they told of their excitement at the flight (it was a first for both of them), and went on to talk about May Day traditions. Afterwards Queen Ann went on to the Royal Orthopaedic Hospital, where she left her bouquet.

Peter Duncan, the BBC producer later wrote to Miss Catt, praising their performance.

Ann was one of the first winners of the Gold Medal at the Hastings Music Festival for her ballet performance. She went on to join the Rosebuds Theatre Company, and stayed a professional dancer until her marriage. She now lives in Wales.

Queen Ann and Mr Knight prepare for the flight (ho)

1949

Queen Valerie Hurcombe

Linton Gardens was the venue again this year, and the 13 year old Valerie Hurcombe was crowned by Councillor Mrs Farnfield. This time it was another historic event, as Mrs Farnfield had just become the first woman Mayor of Hastings.

Valerie, a Bal Edmund School pupil, carried on the new tradition of calling on her subjects to take care of the environment. Miss Godfrey directed the dance.

Miss Catt and Mr Knight carried on their unbroken record of attendance, and the Jack-in-the-Green was in attendance.

A local dancer at the time, now Mrs Collins, remembers the drive to the venue. The May Queen and entourage were taken to Linton Gardens on the back of a coal lorry with the Maypole proudly erect. Unfortunately, the route included a low bridge and disaster was only narrowly avoided when the pole was brought crashing down. No permanent damage was inflicted, but the young ladies were shaken by the event

As an indication of Miss Catt's versatility, this year saw the release of the film of "The Fall of The House of Usher". This was directed by Hastings born George Ivor Barnet and was filmed around Hastings and Fairlight. It starred Gwen Watford and was co-written by Miss Dorothy Catt.

Another, future, May Queen involved was Anne Veness (1953) who, at a very young age, appeared in two scenes.

1950

Queen Shirley Waller

The Mayor, Alderman J.D. Cooper, crowned Shirley Waller at Linton Gardens. 15 year old Shirley lived in Hughenden Road, and may be the first May Queen to come from Hastings and not St Leonards. Councillor Rymill compered the event which included dancing by the Phyliss Godfrey dance school, Orchard School dancers and Sandown Primary School under the direction of Miss Eastham (who the author remembers as one of his teachers at that school). Shirley was a pupil of the Phyllis Godfrey School of dance based at The Hollies in Elphinstone Road. The stage Manager was Mr N. John Cloke, and Miss E.M. Griffiths was, once again, at the piano, ably assisted by Mrs Chantler. As always, Miss Catt directed the whole thing.

Last year's May Queen, Valerie Hurcombe, played the Prince of Merrie England. This is the first mention of this character since 1934, and it was a role that would be replayed for a number of years. The modern concept of Merrie England is of a Victorian blend of nationalistic prejudice and myth. There is, however a school of thought that the word Merrie is derived from the old French, and means "jewel in the sea". Although the phrase is now viewed as a romantic, outdated expression, it was seen in this era as a connection to the May traditions of old. Usually, the Prince of Merrie England was played by the previous May Queen, but in many cases the outgoing queen was of an age where she had left the school, or even the area. So there are occasions when the prince was played by a future queen. The other senior supporter to the May Queen was a Robin Hood. This was a character which had figured in May Day celebrations going back to the late Medieval times, but had not been in the Hastings Pageants since the thirties.

For the first time the shilling given to the May Queen was in the form of a brooch, mounted especially for the ceremony, for the princely sum of nineteen shillings and eleven pence.

Some of the attendants wore tabards from the first Pageant in 1934. These were painted by students of the Hastings College of Art, and showed the quartered arms of Hastings.

1951

Queen Patricia Walsh

For the last time, Linton Gardens was the venue for the Crowning of the May Queen. The Mayor, Alderman Chambers crowned Patricia Walsh of Knotburst Manor, Shirley Drive. She was chosen from the fifty pupils at Bal Edmund School of Dance.

Patricia was met and escorted into the arena by Godfrey West, the Co-Chairman of the Entertainments committee. 14 year old Patricia carried a bouquet of pink and white tulips and was accompanied by Rosie Smart as the Prince of Merrie England. After the Maypole and ballet dancing arranged by Miss Godfrey, there followed "The Masque of Fowers". This was a theatrical dance, arranged by Miss Catt, from a 17th century masque first performed in 1614 at the old Royal Palace in Whitehall.

For the last year or two, the crown had been arranged with fresh flowers by the florist in Queens Arcade, Hastings. This service continued through most of the fifties and early sixties.

Alderman Chambers crowns Queen Patricia (mc)

Queen Patricia enthroned (ho)

For our younger readers, the man in the top left of the previous picture with his back to camera and wearing a white cap is collecting the shillings from the audience for the use of the deckchairs.

In this same year, Battle inaugurated a May Queen Pageant, and Pat Sewett became their first Queen, crowned by Mrs N.E. Nesbit at the Chequers Gardens. It is also noted that a May Queen was crowned "Queen of Beaconsfield Road". This event was one of a handful of these May Queens. Shirley Lawes, the wife of a local historian was an attendant and features in the following photo.

Beaconsfield Road May Queen and entourage in their carnival float

No mention was made in future years about any Beaconsfield May Queens, and it has been suggested that the only reason for this year was that it led to an entry into the Hastings Carnival.

1952

Queen Mary Dutton

The Pageant was switched back to Warrior Square this year, and Mary Dutton was crowned by the Mayor, Alderman Rymill. The event included a "Masque", this time it was simply a parade of children dressed in royal and courtier type dress. Once again, after the dances, the Queen and attendants, were taken (by road) to London to be interviewed on the "In Town Tonight" radio programme. The presenter this time was Cliff Michelmore. Among those in the group was the Prince of Merrie England, Anne Veness, who was to be chosen as next year's Queen.

Mary Dutton now lives in Portugal.

left: Alderman H W Rymill and the sweep escort Mary in the post-crowning tour. (ho)

Right: Queen Mary Dutton (ho)

Pamela Sales, playing Mary Tudor, leads the Masque (mc)

1952

Queen Anne Veness

Finally the Pageant has returned to Alexandra Park. This year has truly a royal theme. The mayor, Alderman Rymill, having crowned Anne Veness declared that he was to attend another coronation in a month's time, that of Queen Elizabeth the second at Westminster Abbey. Even the shilling was of note this year, it being the first Elizabethan shilling given to a Hastings May Queen. Also it was the first time the shilling was presented at the crowning ceremony.

On her arrival, the May Queen was received by Deputy Mayor, Godfrey West. Also in attendance was John Burton the Director of Entertainment. The whole entourage processed around the Lower Lawn arena before Anne took her seat on the Throne.

The crown bearer on the day was Bruce Veness, the May Queen's brother, who went on to become an actor and director at the Stables Theatre. Bruce was only about nine at the time, and was dreadfully embarrassed and upset about having to wear the knickerbockers that went with the costume.

The May Song was sung and the dances followed, performed by Miss Godfrey's school, accompanied by Mrs Griffiths on piano and Mr Percy Stuttle on violin. Although most of the characters were represented, this may be the first year when a "Robin Hood" was not present. The Mayor's speech included the call to care for the flora and fauna.

Anne was a pupil of the Sacred Heart School, but went to both the Bal Edmund and Radcliffe House Orchard Schools. She remembers having a role in a performance of Twelfth Night in the grounds of Bal Edmund. After the Orchard School, Anne went on to dance at Phyliss Godfrey's school. Whilst there she remembers Miss Catt visiting the school one day, and on the following morning she was informed that she had been chosen as May Queen. She progressed through to become a teacher of dance. Later she became the proprietor of the Hastings Stage Studio, which itself has produced several May Queens right through to the new century, and now shares her time between Hastings and France.

Alderman Rymill and his first coronation of 1953 (ho)

It's worth taking note of the costume arrangements at this time, as we have reached the twentieth Hastings May Queen, and those twenty years have seen enormous changes in society and fashions.

The Merrie England, milkmaid, style of dress was becoming a bone of contention with the young ladies, and the mop caps were disliked even more. As it was Miss Catt who supplied the costumes for the Dancers, Flower Girls and Pages, there was not enough money available to change design on a regular basis, but even after twenty years there had been no change. The only sign of modern fashion came with the May Queen's dress. It was always incumbent on the May Queen (or rather, the May Queen's mother) to supply her own dress, and it is here that one can see the difference in the decades.

Ballet shoes or their equivalent have always been worn, even on grass.

The first Elizabethan Shilling presented to Anne (as)

1954

Queen Petrina Cornwell

There was a clash of events for the Mayor this year. On one hand he had the Hastings May Queen, and on the other was the crowning of the Bulverhythe May Queen. As he represented the Bulverhythe Ward it is not surprising he sent his Deputy to Hastings, while he crowned 12 year old Janet Stout as the first Bulverhythe May Queen. In fact, the Mayor crowned two May Queens that day, after Bulverhythe he went immediately to crown another May Queen at Hollington.

Therefore it was Deputy Mayor, Councillor Godfrey West, who crowned Petrina (Trina) Cornwell and presented her with the shilling in Alexandra Park. The Old English and National dances were followed by the winning ballet from the Hastings Music Festival, "Robin Hood". All dances were choreographed by Phyllis Godfrey. Mr Knight collected five guineas in his top hat for the Hastings Old People Welfare Committee.

Before the crowning a recording of the BBC commentary "London's welcome to the Royal Family" from the previous year's coronation, was played.

Petrina went on to become successful in television as a Co-ordinator/ floor manager.

Maypole Dancing 1954 (ho)

Deputy Mayor Godfrey West crowns Petrina (ho)

1955

Queen Angela Burton

On her chauffeured drive to Alexandra Park, the new May Queen, Angela Burton, called in at the home of Mr J Norman Gray to leave her posy of May flowers. Mr Gray was the now-retired Director of Entertainments for Hastings and was convalescing after an illness.

The current Director, Mr John Burton was Angela's father. A few years later Mr Burton went on to become the President of the Hastings Winkle Club, and to receive an MBE. In 1981 he was given the 1066 award by the people of Hastings.

So, Angela (15) was crowned by the Mayor, Alderman FT Hussey, in front of a crowd of nearly 2000 on a beautiful spring day.

Ann Little sang the May Song while the garlands were shown "for pennies".

The Phyllis Godfrey dancers entertained while Mr Knight, now eschewing the idea of selling kisses, took around his hat and collected £4 for the "Old Hastings Preservation Fund" The finale was the dancing of two "plays", George and the Dragon and A Midsummer Night's Dream.

This was another busy year for the Mayor, for he was to be seen later that day crowning the Bulverhythe May Queen. Mr Knight was also pictured at the same event, spreading his luck through the town.

Miss Catt wrote an article for the local paper, in which she talked about the different districts of the Town having become "May Day minded since the late War". These districts being Bulverhythe, Hollington, Ore and Westfield. She mooted the idea of a joint revel, similar to that on Bromley Common, where London's suburban Queens gather and one of them is chosen as the May Queen of London.

She also gave her best wishes for a speedy recovery to Mr Gray as it was his sympathetic interest which led to this annual Pageant.

Queen Angela flanked by the Mayor and Sweep (ho)

The picture below is the only available evidence of the few years that May Queens were selected in Ore Village. The Masonic Hall in Grove Road was the venue for the ceremony.

Dorothy Erends is crowned as the 1955 Ore May Queen

1956

Queen Sylvia Dade

A week before the crowning ceremony, the May Queen elect was taken to London to broadcast on the "In Town Tonight" programme. She was accompanied by Margaret Stretton (nee Hewett), who had been the second Hastings may Queen in 1935.

Fortunately the weather was good and the crowning took place in Alexandra Park with Alderman Hussey, as Mayor, in attendance.

The Bulverhythe and Hollington May Queens had now become established as regular events but the reporting of each event was not as detailed as in previous years. It is known however, that the Hastings event carried on with the same, or similar, format due to the fact that Miss Catt and Miss Godfrey had reached an agreement that their two schools should provide the May Queen on alternate years.

Queen Sylvia tries on the crown for size (ho)

1957

Queen Beverley Cornwell

15 year old Beverley was crowned by Alderman F T Hussey in Alexandra Park.

This was one of the sunniest May Days for the Pageant and a large crowd was on hand to witness the crowning. The Mayor reminded Beverley of her duty to ask her peers to protect the animals and flowers. In her speech, she reflected that she had danced around the Maypole for the last four years and now she was able to watch.The event started with Anne Little singing the children's May song, and after the crowning there followed a ballet piece "The Water Babies" and a Greek ensemble. The Maypole dances finished the afternoon.

Beverley, from Priory Avenue in Hastings went on to teach dance and even directed the dancing for the 1962 May Queen Pageant.

The Hollington May Queen was crowned in a ceremony which included the character of Jack-in-the-Green.

Queen Beverley receives the shilling (ho)

Processing with the Mayor and sweep (ho)

1958

Queen Susan Hyne

This year marked the 25th Hastings May Queen Pageant. In honour of this Miss Catt requested that Henry Burden should perform the crowning. Mr Burden (now Alderman) was the Mayor who crowned Rhona Powell in 1934 at the first Pageant in Warrior Square. Apart from Miss Catt, the only constant participant was Mrs E.M. Grifiths who had played the piano or violin in every one of the 25 Pageants.

Regretfully, rain spoilt the day, as it was "unceasing" throughout the day, and Miss Catt was forced to announce the dancing would have to be postponed to another day.

Andre Martin was the Herald and Ion Castro one of the two Pages. Both of these gentlemen remember the day with affection even if they couldn't remember the exact year!

The crowning of Queen Susan Hyne (ho)

1959

Queen Jennifer Betteridge

1959 proved to be a more clement May Day for the crowning of Jennifer Betteridge by the Mayor, Councillor R.H. Bryant. Alexandra Park was in excellent condition for the ceremony on the Lower Lawn.

The Prince of Merrie England was played by Dawn Mayger, and the Crown Bearer was Ion Castro. Ion's sister, Iona, was one of the maypole dancers. Julian Gibbs was the Herald.

Mrs Griffiths and Mr Baker on violins were joined by Mrs Krikorian on the piano. The Phyllis Godfrey School of Dance provided the entertainment. The speech remained unchanged. As it was written by Miss Catt, it was a lot longer than the modern version and, as Miss Catt was a teacher of elocution, was expected to be read perfectly.

Mr Knight the Chimney Sweep was now known as "the grand old man of May" because of his long association with the Pageant. Councillor Bryant was to be another recipient of the 1066 award (1972)

1960

Queen Deidre Wyatt

An ex- May Queen stole the limelight in Alexandra Park this year. After the Mayor, Councillor R H Bryant, crowned Deidre Wyatt, he went on to present a shilling brooch to Gwen Watford who, by now, had become a nationally celebrated actress of stage and screen. Gwen had been May Queen in 1941, but had not been awarded the gift. This was the chance to rectify that, so 19 years on; she finally received the shilling that was due to her. Gwen had been trained at Miss Catt's speech and drama school.

The weather was the best it had been for many years as 13 year old Deidre was crowned, and presented with her own shilling. Although the fine weather helped, it is an indication of the popularity of the event that it still attracted over 2000 people.

Penelope Rider was the Prince of Merrie England, Andre Martin the page and, of course, Mr Knight was the Sweep. The Pageant followed the usual format with Miss Godfrey's dancers taking centre stage. That evening the event was featured on the news programme on the newly created Southern TV.

Gwen Watford receives her shilling at last. *(ho)*

Councillor Bryant crowns Queen Deidre *(ho)*

Right: Queen Deidre sits on the magnificent throne *(mc)*
This is the best view of Miss Catt's chair that had been used for all the outdoor Pageants.

1961

Queen Margaret White

For the ninth consecutive year the weather was good enough for the Pageant to be held in Alexandra Park although, as in 1958, there was rain. Not enough though to stop the dancing, and the event was carried through, albeit with most of the participants getting damp.

13 year old Margaret White was crowned by the Mayor, Alderman C. Barfoot. The event was introduced by Jane Hills, who sang the Oxfordshire children's May Song. Jane was only 14.and was to be next year's May Queen.

The first Garland competition was held with the Mayor and Mayoress as judges.

Margaret is escorted into the arena by Mr Knight (mc)

The Mayor, crowns Margaret White (ho)

Alderman and Mrs Barfoot judge the Garland competition (mc)

The Court of Queen Margaret (mc)

The 1961 Maypole Dancers (mc)

Pictured above is a remarkable scene as the Park entrance and the crossroads were a lot more open than they are today. In the background is the old Grammar School. Now the area is covered by Saunders Close and Beckett Close, named after two of the "houses" of the old school.

1962

Queen Jane Hills

After a good run in the Park, the Pageant of 1962 was moved to the main hall at the White Rock Pavilion due to bad weather, where Jane Hills was crowned by Alderman C. Barfoot, the Mayor.

Pupils of Miss Phyllis Godfrey performed under the direction of Miss Beverley Cornwell (1957 May Queen). The introductory May Song was sung by Deidre Wyatt, and once again the mayor asked the May Queen to request her subjects to respect wildlife and the flowers of the parks and open spaces.

Jane is the younger sister of Ann the 1948 May Queen, and their niece, Claire, was to be the Queen in 1990. Both Ann and Jane were taught dance by Miss Godfrey Jane went on to act and dance until she married.

Mrs Griffithe, Mr Hayler (violins) and Irene Mitchell (piano) accompanied the dancers.

The Mayor went on to crown the Bulverhythe May Queen, Maureen Boniface at the South Saxons. Several other councillors attended. At Hollington, Patricia Fermor was crowned by TV personality David Clitheroe, and at St Helens the Queen was Iris Wightman.

Alderman Barfoot crowns Queen Jane
(ho)

1963

Queen Petula Portell

The 30th May Queen Pageant in Hastings was celebrated in glorious sunshine in Alexandra Park. The Mayor, Councillor D.W. Wilshin crowned Petula Portell after Deidre Wyatt had sung the May song. The Entertainments Manager, John Burton, welcomed the Mayor and Mayoress. During the procession which had always preceded the enthronement, the characters in 1963 included a Jack-in-the-Green. The sightings of this garlanded figure were very rare at this point and were solely in the province of children. This highlights the difference between the folk memory link to the past traditions, and the more recent local Hastings Jack-in-the-Green festival, which has taken on a vastly different image of the character

Petula went on to have a daughter, who attended Anne Slacke's Hastings Stage Studio.

D W Wilshin crowns Petula Portell (ho)

1964

Queen Rosemary Binge

Bad weather again forced the venue to change to the White Rock. Mayor D.W. Wilshin crowned Rosemary Binge in front of a large audience, after the May Song was sung and the Phyllis Godfrey pupils danced. Ballet had now become an established addition to complement the National and Folk dances.

In Miss Catt's 30th year as director the programme had changed very little, and the characters still included a "Prince of Merrie England", this year it was played by Petula Portell, the previous May Queen.

1965

Queen Linda Glazier

700 people were in the auditorium of the White Rock to watch Councillor Wilshin, the Mayor, crown Linda Glazier (13). Gwenda Bentley was due to sing the May song but fell ill at the last minute, and was replaced by an instrumental version, on recorder, played by Mandy Harrison.

Although the dancing took place, Miss Catt announced she hoped to have a fuller programme at the Park in June for the "At the Court of the May Queen" event. This was to be the first time that this had taken place since the war years.
Once again the Mayor left White Rock to crown the Bulverhythe May Queen, Audrey Cockett, where Sandown Primary School pupils showed their Scottish dancing under the direction of Miss D Young.

At Hollington the May Queen was 11 year old Elaine Harman, and the Deputy Mayor, Councillor Swatland, crowned Marion Piper as the St Helens May Queen.

1966

Queen Yvonne Catt

There is no connection between Miss Catt and this year's May Queen, the name is purely coincidental. Yvonne (14) of Marline Road was a pupil of Miss Catt.

Mr Knight escorts Yvonne into the arena (mc)

The crowning (ho)

In her speech Yvonne reminded the children of the town to take care of the animals and flowers. She also noted the year. This was the 900th anniversary of the Norman Conquest and Hastings was just starting the celebrations which would go on throughout the year. She told the crowd that she wanted to work with children when she left school. By all accounts it was a very good speech which lasted about 10 minutes. This was fairly normal as Miss Catt put a lot of emphasis on the May Queen's speech, and the Queens were chosen for their poise and elocution.

The Prince of Merrie England was Linda Glazier, the May Queen of 1965.

Picture on the left (ho)

Although this photograph is not of good quality, it is worth showing because it is the last picture of William Knight, the Chimney Sweep. It is reported that he was too ill to attend next year's event, and was subsequently not heard of again. So, after 31 May Queen crownings this was to be his last. It is quite possible that we have him to thank for the continuation of one tradition.

Would those children who dressed as Jack-in-the-Green in these Pageants have known about the garlands from their parents, or was the Jack brought to the stage by Bill Knight? Did he come from a Sweeps' family who had a tradition of celebrating May with the Jack? We'll never really know, but we'll remember Mr W.S. Knight with affection.

Miss Catt, however, did celebrate more this year as the previous Sunday marked the 40th anniversary of the Orchard School of Speech and Drama. May Queens of 1943, 1953, 1956 and 1965 were in attendance to celebrate the anniversary. The organiser of the surprise was Anne Veness, the 1953 May Queen, who took Miss Catt and the guests back to her house for the celebration.

One of the few photos of Miss Catt (middle row, centre) (ho)

Another change to the programme was the musician. After attending every one of the 33 Pageants, Mrs Griffiths was replaced by Irene Mitchell. No reason was given, but we hope it was to spend a long and happy retirement.

The Bulverhythe May Queen was crowned by Councillor E.H. Ive, and was attended by the Hollington Queen, Marylin De Silva, who was crowned earlier that day by Deputy Mayor Boutwood. Patricia Davies was crowned St Helens May Queen by Lady Cooper-Key.

1967

Queen Jane Burrows

After the May Song, sung by Tina Hastings accompanied on recorder by Mandy Harrison, Jane Burrows made her entrance into the Alexandra Park arena. On what was the hottest day of the year so far, she was crowned by the Mayor, Councillor D.W. Wilshin.

As mentioned before, Mr Knight was too ill to attend, but there was another major absence as well. The dancers were from the Esme Child school of Dance and the whole event was organised by Miss Child, although overseen by Miss Catt. No further mention was made of Phyllis Godfrey, although she remained a major part of the dance school culture in the town. The Hastings Music and Dance Festival still have various awards in her name, including the Phyllis Godfrey memorial trophy which was presented by Anne Slacke and Pauline Ash. In 1982 Miss Godfrey was to receive the 1066 award from the Borough of Hastings.

So within the space of one year the Pageant lost three important contributors; Mr Knight, Miss Godfrey and Mrs Griffiths, each one had, in their own way, helped to create an enduring tradition.

1968

Queen Alison Hoare

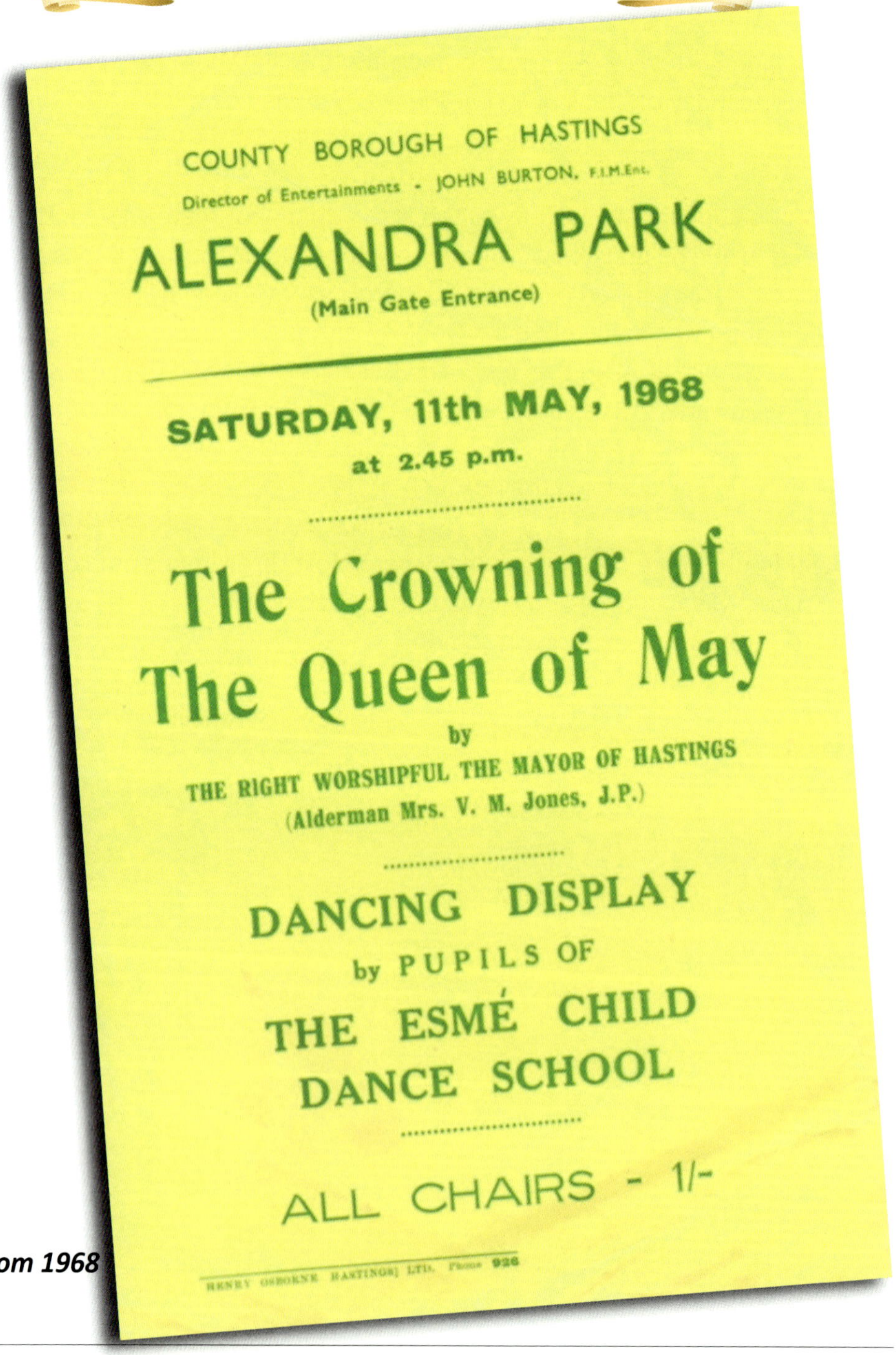

COUNTY BOROUGH OF HASTINGS

Director of Entertainments - JOHN BURTON, F.I.M.Ent.

ALEXANDRA PARK

(Main Gate Entrance)

SATURDAY, 11th MAY, 1968
at 2.45 p.m.

The Crowning of
The Queen of May

by

THE RIGHT WORSHIPFUL THE MAYOR OF HASTINGS

(Alderman Mrs. V. M. Jones, J.P.)

DANCING DISPLAY
by PUPILS OF
THE ESMÉ CHILD
DANCE SCHOOL

ALL CHAIRS - 1/-

HENRY OSBORNE (HASTINGS) LTD. Phone 926

A flier from 1968

The Mayor, Mrs Vera Jones, crowns Alison Hoare (ho)

A good sized crowd in Alexandra Park for the crowning this year even though the weather was not as good as last year. A watery sun and cold wind made it uncomfortable for the participants, Tina Hastings sang the May Song, accompanied by Mandy Harrison on recorder.

The garlands for pennies were shown, and the pupils of Esme Child danced around the Maypole and finished with a dancing display.

1969

Queen Jeanette Vidler

14 year old Jeanette of Plynlimmon Road attended the Hastings Secondary School for girls on Rye Road. For the last two years she was also a pupil of Miss Catt's Orchard School. She was crowned by the Deputy Mayor, Alderman G H Tanner.

For the first time the Pageant was not reported in the local newspaper. Only the above picture with one paragraph was printed the week before the event took place. This may have something to do with the fact that the Mayor, John Hodgson, was crowning his niece as the Bulverhythe May Queen. This was fully covered by the paper.

(ho)

Also the St Helens May Queen was being crowned by the prospective parliamentary candidate, Kenneth Warren, which was also well reported. The reduction in coverage by the local "Observer" becomes more pronounced over the next few years as we move into a more "progressive" era when traditions and all things non-modern are shunned by society.

1970

Queen Gail Benet

Due to a bitterly cold wind and very damp grass from heavy rain the day before, the Pageant was moved to the White Rock Pavilion. Alderman G.H. Tanner, the mayor, crowned 13 year old Gail Benet. Gail, in common with most May Queens, had been involved with the Maypole dancing for a number of years and as attendant before that.

The May Song was sung by Elizabeth Hancox, and the Prince of Merrie England was Susan Robinson. Esme Child's Dance School pupils danced. The May Queen's speech included the, now traditional, call to the children to respect the animals and plants.

Alderman Tanner crowns Queen Gail (ho)

1971

Queen Deborah Burden

Although cold and overcast, Alexandra Park played host to this year's Pageant. The Mayor (E.P. Nye) was unavailable, so Alderman Dawson crowned Deborah Burden. Esme Child's pupils were on hand to dance, and the traditional "garlands for pennies" were taken round.

The local newspaper coverage was, again, virtually non-existent. This reflects the lack of interest from both the public in what was seen as an archaic tradition, and from the Council as an irrelevance to the modern priorities of the Town.

May Queen elect Deborah pictured with
May blossom before the crowning (ho)

Alderman Dawson crowns Queen Deborah (ho)

1972

Queen Angela Wren

This year, the weather won out and the Pageant returned to the wet weather venue of the White Rock. Mayor, Alderman Farley-Paine crowned Angela Wren with due ceremony. Angela was the daughter of the Jeweller who had a shop in Queens Arcade, Hastings.

With Miss Catt still in charge after 38 years, the format remained roughly the same. One addition this year was a competition for the best dressed basket.

The Bulverhythe event was also hit by the weather. 12 year old Sharon Weller was crowned by Deputy Mayor Darker at the Church of The Holy Redeemer hall.

1973

Queen Judith Anne Cresswell

Although only 14, Judith Anne Cresswell had been involved with the Pageant for eight years. Fittingly she was to be the Queen this year.

The venue was Alexandra Park, and for only the third time the May Queen was not crowned by a Mayor or Mayoress. This time the honour fell to Miss Gwen Watford, who was by now a famous celebrity in film and theatre.

Miss Esme Child's pupils performed the dances, but the event was still run by Miss Catt, now in her 39th year and 40th May Queen as organiser.

The Mayor, Alderman Tom Mears, was at the crowning of the Bulverhythe May Queen, 12 year old Lisa Knowlton. Run by the Bulverhythe Childrens Association, the event featured the De Havillande Dance Troupe.

1974

Queen Carolyn Nash

The 1974 May Queen Pageant must have been the most emotional of all. Miss Catt directed her 41st event in 40 years since starting the tradition in 1934.

Everything was there including Esme Child's pupils with ballet and folk dancing. The Maypole dancing, garlands for pennies and all the characters. Robin Hood, the Prince of Merrie England, the Heralds, the Crown Bearer, the Standard Bearer, the Train Bearer, Maids of Honour and all the attendants were on view.

Fortunately it was a warm, sunny day for the crowning, in Alexandra Park, of 12 year old Carolyn Nash. At Miss Catt's request the crowning was performed by John Burton, the Director of Entertainment for Hastings, who had been involved with the event for many years. This may have been a genuine tribute to the work done by Mr Burton, but is it possible that, as the Town had just elected its first Labour Mayor, Miss Catt was showing some prejudice? Who knows?

Miss Catt had a few surprises that Saturday afternoon. Five previous May Queens arrived to celebrate with her. Mary Dutton, Anne Veness, Angela Burton, Beverley Cornwell and Angela Wren were the May Queens of 1952/53/54/58 and 1972. Anne Veness (now Anne Slacke) had arranged an after event celebration at her home.

Queen Carolyn with the dancers (ho)

Although Miss Catt continued to have some involvement with the May Queen Pageant, this is her final year as Director. Without her research and hard work all those years ago, Hastings would not have a traditional May Queen Pageant which has links to the original festival that Ruskin envisioned in 1881, and is still going strong into the twenty first century.

Miss Dorothy Catt and May Queens past and present (ho)

1975

Queen Heather Alexander

Not exactly a surprise, but quite a present for Heather Alexander as she became the Hastings May Queen on her 14th birthday. She did not have far to travel as, at the time, she lived in Upper Park Road.

Crowned by Deputy Mayor Jack Cook in Alexandra Park, Heather also became the first Hastings May Queen after the reign of Miss Catt. This year the Pageant was directed by Miss Esme Child. This is not to say that Miss Catt disappeared from the scene, she was to have some influence over the choosing of May Queens for the next few years as she continued her work at the Orchard School of Speech and Drama.

Although under new direction, the format followed familiar lines. The Oxfordshire May song started the event and the garlands were taken round by the attendants "for pennies". Ballet and folk dancing preceded the Maypole dances. All performed by pupils of Miss Child.

The most obvious sign of a sea-change in the Pageant was the loss of the "Merrie England" style dresses of the dancers and attendants. Miss Child introduced the new, plainer, classic style which was to last for the next thirty four years. The image of the participants evolved from the floral eighteenth century shepherdess to a plainer stylised, dance school version.

1976

Although crowd numbers were diminishing, several hundred people turned out to see Elaine Waller crowned by the Mayor, Councillor John Alexandra Park. Heather Alexander, last year's Queen, was her escort as the Prince of Merrie England. To emphasise Miss Catt's continued presence, Elaine was a pupil of her school, and was chosen by her to be Queen. Although the Maypole dances were performed by Miss Child's pupils, the dancing displays were by the Vivienne Moore School of Dance.

It was noted at the time that Elaine's Mother must have spent a fortune on the dress. It was described as "magnificent" and included a huge train.

Unusually for the time, the May Queen had another appointment this year, as she was asked to open the Westfield village fete.

Queen Elaine is crowned by Councillor Hodgson (mc)

Queen Elaine opens the Westfield village fete

1977

Queen Henrietta Hammet

Alexandra Park was bathed in bright sunshine for the crowning of Henrietta Hammet by the Deputy Mayor, Councillor Frank Jones.

Part of the speech by the Mayor had, by now, become a tradition. Councillor Chamber's request that the new May Queen ask her subjects, the young people of Hastings, to respect and care for the wildlife and environs of the town, was used almost every year since 1946. This year was no exception.

The dance display as well as the Maypole dances was performed by the Vivienne Moore School of Dance.

Queen Henrietta is crowned by Councillor Jones (ho)

The Bulverhythe May Queen event did not fare so well this year. The voting had taken place and 12 year old Janet Ayres had been selected. However, later that evening the votes were checked and it was found that 13 year old Karen Boniface should have been chosen. After a hastily convened meeting, the committee agreed to let the original decision stand and to keep Janet as Queen. Threats to resign and arguments raged. The hero of the hour was James Boniface, Karen's father who gracefully accepted that, although his daughter should have been chosen, it would have been too cruel to take the crown away from Janet after she had been given it. The crowning took place on Jubilee day 7th June.

At the Hastings Music and Dance Festival of this year an earlier May Queen, Gwen Watford, presented the Dorothy Catt Trophy for the best pair of dramatic performances (of which one is from Shakespeare)

1978

Queen Janet West

Very little information is available for this year, a trend that continued through the seventies and eighties. 16 year old Janet West, of Amherst Close, was crowned by the Mayor, Councillor Frank Jones, at the White Rock Pavilion.

We do know, however, that this was the year that an Act of Parliament gave us the right to a further Bank Holiday on the first Monday in May.

Queen Janet's coronation

Queen Janet with Councillor Jones (ho)

1979

Queen Caroline Bruce

Another rain-affected day meant the White Rock was the venue for this year's Pageant. The Mayor, Councillor John Hodgeson, crowned 15 year old Caroline Bruce.

The Cinders Dance School entertained the relatively small audience with six set dances, and Sally Woodward was the May Queen's attendant. Caroline and Sally were good friends, and Caroline remembers them practising disco dancing in her bedroom.

Caroline was a pupil of Miss Esme Child, and was sent, along with two other pupils, to Miss Catt in order to read to her. It was the elocution and deportment of the young ladies which determined who was to be May Queen, beauty was a secondary consideration. After Caroline was chosen, she then had to attend upon Miss Catt another two or three times to go through the

Caroline and Sally set out for the White Rock (cb)

speech. As Caroline admitted, Miss Catt taught her to "elongate her vowels".

The speech had always been memorised, and the May Queens were not allowed to hold a copy from which to read. It was a daunting task as these speeches were usually two pages long and after the initial delight of being chosen, Caroline said she was extremely nervous of the ordeal of making the speech. Combined with the fact that, having only just started a Saturday job at Woolworth's in Hastings and she had to ask for the time off, the whole day was a mixture of pleasure and tension for a young girl.

Caroline and attendants on the white Rock stage (cb)

Caroline's dress was made and fitted for her by a local lady who was experienced in dressmaking for the dance schools, and after the event was given to the school for use by future queens.

In July of this year the May Queen attended the local carnival.

1980

Queen Teresa Woodhouse

Now becoming lower key, the Pageant had smaller audiences and a low priority as far as the local paper was concerned. Hence the apparent lack of information. We do know that Teresa Woodhouse, a Maplehurst School pupil, was crowned by John Hodgson in Alexandra Park. The dancers were from the Cinders school of dance, and the Mayor and Mayoress judged a garland competition. This is probably the first time that Miss Child directed the Pageant alone. Little is known about the involvement of Miss Catt at this time. Apart from being instrumental in choosing the May Queens, there did not seem to be a specific role for her.

1981

Queen Amanda Rapp

Chosen by Miss Catt, Amanda Rapp was crowned by the mayor, Councillor Bernard Spray. The event, being rain affected, was held at the White Rock. Amanda's twin sister, Samantha, was the Prince of Merrie England and Mr Bob Pettit was the attending sweep.

Queen Amanda with Mr Pettit
(ho)

1982

Queen Samantha Rapp

Samantha Rapp was crowned at the White Rock and her twin, Amanda, was to be the prince in a mirror image of the previous year. Unfortunately, Amanda was stricken with an asthma attack and was unable to attend. The part of the prince was taken by Wendy Thornton who was to play an important role in the Pageant for the next two years.

Another former director, Miss Phyllis Godfrey was given this year's 1066 award by Hastings Council.

Miss Catt had chosen the twins and said "you couldn't find two more beautiful girls". A fitting tribute to the two girls. They were the last to be chosen to be the May Queen of Hastings by the creator of the event.

49 years after the crowning of Rhona Powell, this was to be Miss Catt's final involvement with the May Queen. With little or no ceremony, the Pageant slipped into a new era and left behind all connections with the characters and style of the past.

Queen Samantha Rapp (ho)

1983

The 50th Hastings May Queen, Wendy Thornton was 16 when the Mayor, Councillor Alan Stace crowned her in Alexandra Park. This year the May Queen was selected by Miss Child and so a new era began.

Queen Wendy, Mr Pettit and Crown Bearer Robert Golding (wt)

A kiss for the Queen (ho)

1984

Queen Wendy Thornton

In an unusual turn of events, Wendy Thornton became the May Queen for the second year running. This time she was crowned at the White Rock by Councillor Stace as the weather was abysmal.

The official reason for this repeat crowning was that she did not have time to carry out her duties for the year. A strange declaration, because few May Queens have ever had more than two or three appearances to make during their term of office.

However, the real reason was the infighting amongst the prospective May Queens' mothers. There were two main contenders for the crown this year, and the mothers of these two were becoming vociferous and had started to pressurise Miss Child. Miss Child finally became exasperated by the constant arguments and expectations of these two and, in order to teach them a lesson, declared that neither of them would be Queen. In case of any retribution against a new Queen, she asked Wendy to reprise her role from the previous year. So Wendy Thornton is the only person to have in her possession two of the shilling brooches given by Hastings council.

1985

Queen Emma Coulman

Again the poor weather dictated an indoor venue. As the White Rock had been booked for another event, the Pageant was held at the Falaise Hall. Emma Coulman was crowned by the Deputy Mayor, Councillor David Thornton. The fourth year in a row where a Thornton had played a part, but he was not related to Wendy. Emma was a pupil of the Hastings Stage Studio.

Miss Child directed, the sweep was Mr Pettit and the Wendy Cameron dance school pupils performed.

1986

Queen Emma Stace

Another year at the White Rock. For the fifth time in nine years the weather had taken its toll. 15 year old Emma Stace was crowned by Deputy Mayor John Hodgson.

Emma was another May Queen who attended the Hastings Stage Studio. As her mother was a teacher of music it is not so surprising that Emma went on to be an Opera singer. She now lives in Italy.

Miss Child had decided to move to Doncaster for family reasons, and had asked Miss Irene Spillett to take over responsibility for the Pageant. This year Miss Spillett was still working alongside Miss Child but was to take over full control next year.

So this was to be Miss Child's twelfth and last Pageant.

For the first time in many years the Council's face of the Pageant was named. He was Glen Crocker, who had the grand title of Assistant Resort Services Manager. Whereas the representatives of the Council in the past had taken a more active role, in recent years the "Entertainments Managers" or Tourism Executives were just there to facilitate the Pageant. After Norman Gray (1934-1944) E.W. Clements, H.C.Burgess, Alderman Rymill and John Burton, the staging of the Pageant was left to the likes of Miss Catt and her successors. The Council backed the event, but without a direct involvement, other than the Mayor's crowning role, although it is noticeable that this role had recently been delegated to the Deputy Mayor. The enthusiasm of the council had begun to wane. This was reflected in the local newspapers as there was a distinct lack of coverage through the eighties and into the nineties.

1987

Queen Nicola Rodmell

Described as a "dancing starlet", 16 year old Nicola Rodmell was crowned as the 54th Hastings May Queen, in Alexandra Park.

Nicola was a pupil of the Hastings Stage Studio.

Miss Irene Spillett was now in sole charge and was to direct the next 23 Pageants. As she had studied at the London College of Dance and Drama, and as part of her teacher training, had studied Morris Dance and traditions, she was well placed to take on the role.

Mad Jack's Morris was asked to continue their support of the Pageant and performed their dances as well as leading the procession into the arena. They also re-introduced the display of garlands.

Bob Pettit was the Chimney Sweep and the Ambury and Silverlea dance schools' pupils performed ballet and gymnastics.

Miss Spillett was to continue the practise devised by Miss Child when choosing a May Queen. Miss Child's criteria included; good deportment, accomplished speaking, age 15-18years and locally based, or with local contact. These criteria were based on Miss Catt's original ideas.

1988

Queen Lisa Walters

There seems to be a fresh new look to the event around this era. The word Pageant no longer appears to be appropriate. Instead, the event becomes more of a staged show, and more in tune with the modern culture.

When Lisa Walters was crowned by the Lady Mayor, Sandie Barr, in Alexandra Park, the Maypole dancing was the highlight. The only other form of dance was a set performed by the Mad Jack's Morris side.

For the first time since 1936, the event took place without a Chimney sweep. There is no indication why Mr Pettit did not attend, but as he was not there it would have been difficult for Miss Spillett to find a replacement due to the reduction in the numbers of Sweeps in the area. Modern forms of heating meant that the only Sweep in the area was in Bexhill. Hastings was not to have its own Sweep for another four years.

By now the whole event was under threat. The lack of coverage in the local paper was an indication of the apathy from the council for this event. There was even talk amongst some council members of scrapping the event altogether and The Crowning of the Hastings May Queen was close to becoming extinct. In fact, if the Jack-in-the-Green celebrations of May Day had not started to become so popular, the chances of continuing past the next couple of years were very slim.

1989

Queen Heidi Welsh

Unknown at the time, this was to be the last May Queen Event in Alexandra Park for 24 years.

Heidi Welsh was crowned by The Mayor, Sandie Barr, and the pupils of the Irene Spillett School of Dance danced the Maypole, followed by Mad Jack's Morris. Heidi was a pupil of the Hastings Stage Studio.

The following ten years will show how the pageant had become diminished in the Hastings calendar of events. From the conception in 1934 until the eighties there was an enthusiasm within the town for the tradition, but the lack of interest within the Council, and little (in some cases no) reporting by the local papers, meant that the 90's were the least positive decade for the event. Miss Spillett must be acknowledged for her perseverance and, in the last few years of her tenure, for her strength of character in continuing the tradition through a debilitating illness, which meant that she organised, rehearsed and compered the whole thing alone and in pain.

1990

Queen Claire Hills

A new era dawns with the use of Hastings Castle as a venue. Over the last few years the Hastings Traditional Jack-in-the-Green festival had grown beyond recognition, and had become reliant on Council sponsorship to exist in its current form. This included the use of Hastings Castle for the finale on the Monday. The outlay from the Council was, and is, significant for the use of the Castle, as safety regulations required many changes and additions to existing arrangements to accommodate the numbers of people watching. Consequently, it was deemed appropriate to use the already erected stage and tea tent for the May Queen event. The organiser, Irene Spillet was agreeable as she saw the benefits of being associated with the Jack-in-the-Green weekend.

So Claire Hills became the first of many May Queens to be crowned in Hastings Castle. The Official was the Deputy Mayor, June Fabian. The Irene Spillett School dancers performed the Maypole Dances, and Mad Jack's Morris appeared on stage.

Claire was eighteen years old when she was crowned, but already had an impressive pedigree. She started at the Vivienne Moore School of dance at the age of three. She went to Miss Godfrey's school when she was six and Laton Ash School of dance from age ten to thirteen. From there she attended the Elmhurst Ballet School and, at seventeen, taught dance at Miss Spillett's school. Claire went on to teach music.

In retrospect, it is now quite obvious that this venue drastically changed the event. The Castle is difficult to get to by car compared to the Park, and its location took the event out of the awareness of the public. Although the glorious weather of 1990 meant that the Castle was packed with people, in later years the audience numbers dropped to a mere couple of hundred at best, and the programme was cut to a minimum of dances.

Queen Claire, her Mother and grandmother *(jh)*

This was to be a particularly good year for Claire. Before being named as May Queen, she had won a Gold Medal at the Hastings Music Festival.

Claire now lives in Hong Kong and has six children.

The above picture shows the May Queen dress that Miss Spillett introduced in 1987. None of the girls liked it, but it remained in service until 2010.

1991

Queen Debbie Martin

Not such a sunny day for the crowning of Debbie Martin. Debbie was a pupil of Helenswood School and of the Ambury Dance School. She was 16 when she was crowned, but had attended the Pageants from the age of 4, first as a flower girl then becoming a dancer. Mad Jack's Morris headed the procession of the May Queen elect, through heavy rain.

The Crown Bearer was six year old Lewis St John, and the Standard bearer was Richard Beale (11).

Queen Debbie valiantly ignores the rain (ho)

1992

Queen Natalie Driver

The crowning of 16 year old Natalie was a poorly reported event, warranting only two lines in the local newspaper. Consequently this was another year about which little is known. The background to the picture below shows that the event was held in the Castle, and we do know that Mad Jack's Morris danced after the ceremony.

(ho)

1993

Queen Charlotte Lord

Regretfully, apart from the name of the May Queen, nothing is known about this year.

This was a real shame, as there are no details to report of the sixtieth Hastings May Queen crowning

1994

Queen Emma Hardy

By now the Castle had become established as the venue for the event, and after five years away from Alexandra Park, there was a difference to the public perception of a May Queen.

Because of the association with the Jack-in-the-Green festival, the Crowning of the May Queen had been reduced to being just one of a number of events taking place over the Bank Holiday weekend. A lot of people were beginning to view the festival as a somewhat ribald, raucous and almost pagan event and the link between the Jack and the May Queen was emphasised in the advertising and reporting of them both. Thus we enter the era of the May Queen crowning being perceived by some as a pagan ritual.

So when 16 year old Emma Hardy was crowned by Deputy Mayor, Gladys Stewart the small crowd and relaxed atmosphere showed how far the event had come from the days of Miss Catt.

On a sunny day, the entertainment began with a re-enactment of an assault on Hastings Castle by the Sussex Company of Armed Militia. Inside the Castle, the fun was provided by Mad Jack's Morris before the ceremony, followed by the maypole dances.

The format for the castle was for the participants to process into the arena from a starting point by the changing tent. This was situated just 50 yards away, so the procession, comprising 25 participants and Mad Jack's Morris, was minimal and short lived.

Emma's dress was one that Miss Spillett had supplied to all her May Queens, but the train had been made by Emma's mother, Pam, who then donated it to the future May Queens. Emma's sister, Kay, had danced at several Pageants and observed that, with a stiff breeze, the ribbons were extremely difficult to hold. This was another of the problems of the Castle as a venue, the exposure to the elements.

Emma went on to become a teacher.

Our thanks go to Stuart and Pam Hardy, Emma's parents, for the information about this year.

Another feature of this year was the crowning of the first Hollington May Queen since 1966.

Queen Emma Hardy (ho)

1995

Queen Anna-Leigh Glover

A special year for the author. A new sweep was introduced to the event and 1995 saw Barry Jones join the Pageant.

Anna-Leigh Glover was crowned in Hastings Castle by the Mayor, Councillor Richard Stevens.

Irene Spillet directed the event and the pupils from her school performed the Maypole dances. A children's Garland competition was held.

Queen Anna-Leigh and entourage (ho)

Mike Marsh was the Tourism manager who arranged the Council's promotion of the event.

1996

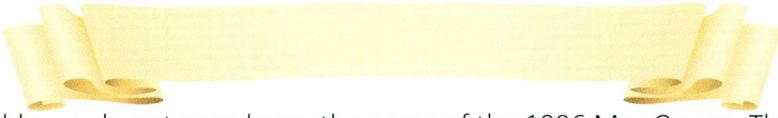

Unbelievably, we do not even know the name of the 1996 May Queen. There were now two newspapers in Hastings. The "Observer" and the free paper, "The Adnews", (previously The Hastings News). Neither paper covered the event, so the continuity of information has been lost. We would welcome any information from our readers, who may know more than we do.

1997

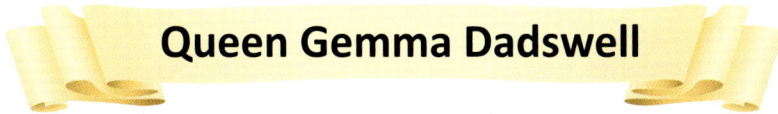

Queen Gemma Dadswell

Constant rain and high wind managed to disrupt the Morris dancing throughout the town. The Jack-in-the-Green festival had taken to the hostelries of the Old Town. The May Queen and entourage however carried on. With a quick Maypole dance of just 2 or 3 minutes, Gemma Dadswell was crowned. For only the second time the May Queen was crowned by somebody from outside the Council. The Group Editor of the Hastings Observer, Peter Lindsey did the honours. Due to the weather, 1997 probably holds the record for the smallest audience, with the numbers counted in dozens rather than hundreds.

The only official attendee was Sandra Barrett of the Borough Tourism Department

The young Flower Girl with the red waist band in front of Gemma is the daughter of the 1990 May Queen, Claire Fletcher (nee Hills). Alice Fletcher was three at the end of that May, and went on to get a BA (hons) degree in Musical Theatre at Guildford University.

Queen Gemma and entourage braving the elements (ho)

Peter Lindsey crowns Queen Gemma under the hastily erected tent (ho)

1998

Queen Katie Chenery

Once again, lack of local newspaper coverage means that we have no details for this year. The only mention of Katie is in the following year's programme, where she is shown as the "outgoing May Queen".

Mentioned for the first time was Mr Kevin Boorman from the Borough Tourism Department

1999

Queen Elizabeth Salt

One of the most popular Mayors of Hastings in the last thirty years, Godfrey Daniel, crowned Elizabeth Salt in Hastings Castle. On one of the warmer May Day weekends for some time, the crowd was much larger than it had been for the past six years, probably approaching around two hundred. A notable addition to the proceedings was the Town Crier, Jon Bartholomew. Barry Jones the Chimney Sweep was there, along with the Page Boy (Oliver Dale) and the Train Bearer, Kirsty Whittington, who went on to become May Queen in 2004.

THE CROWNING OF THE QUEEN OF MAY

HASTINGS CASTLE
WEST HILL
SUNDAY, 2ND MAY 1999
COMMENCING AT 2.00 P. M

AN AFTERNOON OF MUSIC AND DANCE
PRESENTED BY IRENE SPILLETT
REFRESHMENTS AND FULL BAR

The new-style programme

2000

After sixty six years this is one year without a May Queen. Instead, in order to mark the new century, it was decided to create the;

Millennium Prince and Princess

After a prior competition during what was called the "Millennium Weekend", Josef Stout (16) and Eugenie Demeza (14) were crowned by the Mayor, Godfrey Daniel at Hastings Castle. They were chosen from a strong group of contenders by the Mayor and Observer Editor, Richard Neale.

On hand to lead the procession into the arena was the "Lucky Sweep", Barry Jones and Jon Bartholomew, the Town Crier.

Jo Deeprose was the "Lady in waiting" Attendants were Elizabeth Grain and Millie Jeffries, and the Page Boy was Jac Darby.

Prince Josef and Princess Eugenie
(ho)

After the ceremony Irene Spillet's dancers' performed the Maypole dancing, and Mad Jack's danced the Morris.

Also in attendance was the 4 month old daughter of Barry Jones, Bethan, who was to go on to be a Flower Girl, Attendant, Dancer and eventually May Queen over the next 15 years.

2001

Queen Abigail Shillabeer

Going back to a lower key ceremony after the Millennium Pageant, the Mayor crowned Abigail Shillabeer at the Castle. 15 year old Abigail was a pupil of Filsham Valley School. Although the sun shone the wind was blustery.

A new addition to the Pageant was the two Shetland ponies "Magic" and "Sheergar" and the Trap upon which the May Queen entered the arena. She was preceded by the Sweep, Town Crier and the Mayor.

Queen Abigail descends from her carriage (ho)

Owing to the success and growth of the Jack-in-the-Green festival, the local paper's coverage of the event increased, and more of the May Queen pageant was beginning to be captured on film.

2001 attendants (ho)

2002

Queen Siobhan Steuart-Pownell

As previously stated, over the last few years the audience numbers had decreased. However, a good crowd of about 200 saw Siobhan Steuart- Pownel crowned by Deputy Mayor Phil Scott at the Castle.

Queen Siobhan with flower girls Victoria and Hanni Coleman (ho)

The procession was led into the arena by the Town Crier and Chimney Sweep. Although only about 50 yards from the girls' changing tent to the arena, the May Queen rode on the trap pulled by Magic the pony, followed by the flower girls and dancers from Irene Spillett's Ambury School.

For the first time in 68 years the Maypole dancers included boys. Nathan Vaughan-Harris, Luke Botting and Tom Wickens became the first male dancers. Although boys were present for the next 2 years, the dancers soon reverted to being girls only, until 2010/11 when Alfie and Charlie Pitt were "persuaded" to perform

2003

Queen Nicola Martin

One year on, and Phil Scott, in his new role as Mayor, crowns Nicola Martin at the Castle. With the same format as before, the only addition to the cast was a Storyteller, Ben Fairlight.

The number of male dancers was increased to six, becoming the highest of any year before, or since. Dancing around the Maypole were three future May Queens for 2006, 2008 and 2009.

Once again, a limited amount of coverage meant that little else is known of this year. Fortunately, this is probably the last time the event would be allowed to be overlooked by the media.

2004

Queen Kirsty Whittington

For the third year in a row, and the second as Mayor, Phil Scott crowned the May Queen. This time it was 16 year old Kirsty Whittington. Kirsty was another who had been involved for many years with the Pageant. She was Train Bearer in 1999.

The Sweep and Town Crier were joined again by Ben Fairlight with Hannah's Cat dancing the Morris.

It is not known for certain, but this is probably the year that Hannah's Cat Women Morris took over as the regular accompanying Morris side. Mad Jack's men had appeared previously, but did not empathise with the event, seeing it more as a duty to support the May Queen as part of the Jack-in-the-Green weekend. Hannah's Cat, led by Heather Leech, however became immersed in the tradition, and went on to become an integral part of the day and vital to its continuation. At one point they introduced an "It's a knockout" style competition to induce visiting Morris sides to attend the event but even the Castle was seen as too far away from all the activities in the Old Town to attract many of the dancers.

Queen Kirsty and her entourage (ho)

2004 Maypole dancers (ho)

So it was becoming obvious that, unless the crowning took place in the Old Town, the May Queen ceremony was not seen by the Jack-in-the-Green participants as one of their activities, although the public perceived it to be so.

2004 Flower Girls (ho)

Another item of interest is the evolution of the flower girls. They have, for some years, carried small decorative baskets of flowers, which is a representation of the garlands of old which were shown "for pennies" as a way of raising money for charity.

2005

Queen Anna-Marie Kimber

A day of blue sky and warm sunshine greeted 17 year old Anna-Marie Kimber at the Castle. She was crowned by the Mayor, Councillor Pam Brown. Anna was planning to attend stage school, but said that this day made her a "tiny bit nervous because it was a real honour to be chosen"

In another connection between the May Queens, Anna-Marie is the niece of Nicola Rodmell (1987).

Since 2003 Miss Spillett had been forced to use a portable cassette recorder to play the music for the dancers. Ian Dobson, a local sound engineer, had been brought in by the Council to arrange speakers and microphone, and had managed to perform miracles in making the

Queen Anna-Marie (ho)

music acceptable. It was, however, very tinny and false, so it was a welcome new development to have live music this year. A young local violinist called Holly Sheldrake was brought in. Holly was heavily involved in the local folk scene and went on to record albums with The Climax Ceilidh Band. She was able to introduce the more appropriate music for the introduction and Maypole dancing

The Storyteller, Ben Fairlight *(ho)*

2006

Queen Alison Frencer

Councillor Pam Brown, the Mayor, crowned Alison Frencer at the Castle. Ever reliable, Jon Bartholomew, as Town Crier, was beginning to take a more responsible role in gently directing the Mayors through the event, and ensuring the "pomp" of the Pageant was maintained. The one sad moment came in the report by the local Observer, when it described the event as an ancient pagan ceremony. This indicated just how much the Pageant had slipped from the consciousness of the general public, and how it had become just a small part of the Jack-in-the-Green festival. The reporting and photographs were included in a report of the whole weekend and consequently were limited in scope.

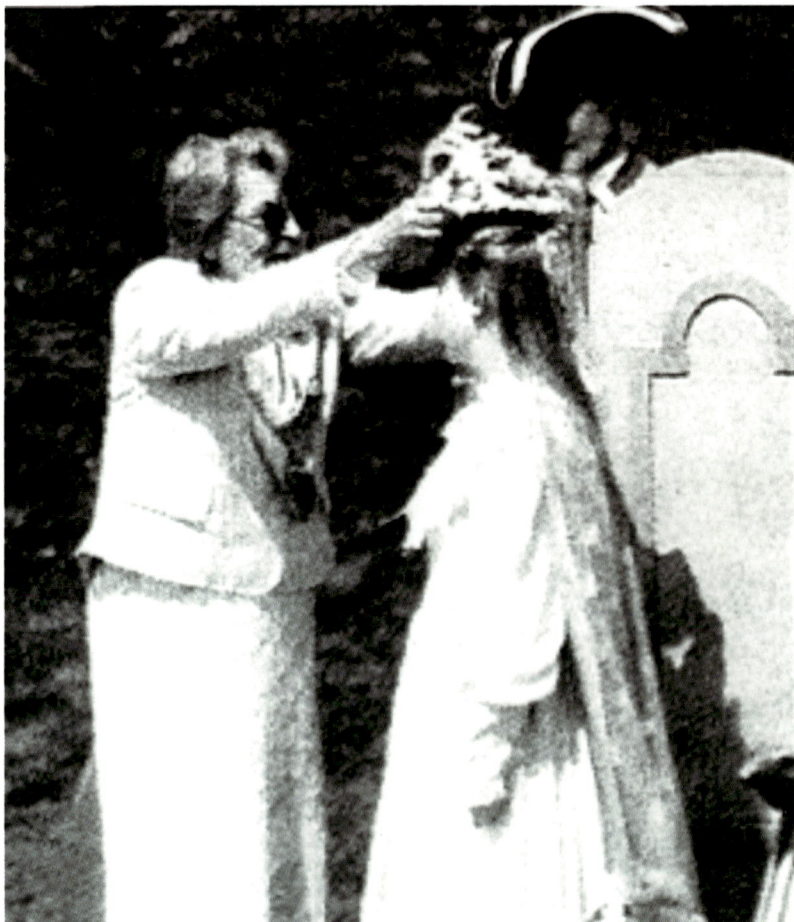

Councillor Pam Brown crowns Queen Alison (ho)

Queen Alison and entourage (ho)

2006 Flower Girls *(ho)*

2007

Queen Ashley Rudd

Ashley Rudd had been a flower girl in 1999, and now she was crowned as May Queen by the former Mayor, Councillor Godfrey Daniel.

Queen Ashley gives her speech (ho)

After a request from Holly Sheldrake, the decision was made to allow her to bring in her "Fiddle Choir". There was some debate about the competence of this new group of amateur musicians whom Holly had been teaching. As a party to this discussion, I was enthusiastic about them, as I saw the event as something which should be far from "professional" and should be from the heart and not the purse. Fortunately I was right, as they turned out to be perfect for the event. (That's not to say that they didn't make a few mistakes in their first year – I'm sure they won't mind me saying that), and have been a popular feature ever since.

2008

Queen Michaela Botting

Another "veteran", Michaela Botting was involved with the May Queen Pageant since she was a three year old Flower Girl. Now 16, she was crowned by the Mayor, Councillor Pam Brown. This was to be one of Councillor Brown's last appointments before her retirement.

Queen Michaela (ho)

As seen in the above picture, it was one of the nicest May afternoons in the Castle, although a stiff breeze kept things on the cool side.

Magick the pony pulled the Queen into the arena

It should be noted that this year's event was the tenth overseen on behalf of the council by Kevin Boorman. Since the mid-sixties the council Tourism/Entertainment managers have not had any impact on the event and it had just managed to stay alive by the enthusiasm of the organisers and participants. Since 1998, when Kevin took up the role, there appears to have been a new strength to the event, and council support has reappeared.

Some of the Hannah's Cat side, with Heather Leech on the throne dreaming of being a May Queen someday. (ho)

2009

Queen Victoria Coleman

In front of the biggest crowd for the May Queen in the Castle, Victoria Coleman was crowned by the Mayor.

Around 400 people watched the crowning, Maypole dancing and Hannah's Cat Morris Ladies.

Queen Victoria can be seen dancing on the extreme left of the group (ic)

This was to be Miss Spillett's last year as organiser of the Pageant. Due to ill health she found it difficult to carry on. As she was solely responsible for the organising, rehearsals, the presentation and being MC it is not surprising it had become impossible to maintain the excellence she demanded. Thus the days of the Dance School proprietor as the driving force behind the Pageant drew to a close. Since 1934 these technically brilliant (and formidable) Ladies had designed and carried on a tradition that we still want to see today. But times change and the Pageant has evolved into something less formal, as have most things in modern life.

Miss Spillett was to say later that she felt honoured to be asked to arrange this event, as she felt she and her pupils were representing the Town in celebrating May Day.

The Hastings Music Festival has a cup awarded in her name for the highest marks for under 12's in the Greek dance class.

2010

Queen Bethany Hill

After the departure of Irene Spillett, the Council's Marketing Manager, Kevin Boorman, asked Barry Jones and his wife Helen if they would be prepared to take on the role of organising the Pageant. Both were members of the Jack-in-the Green committee, and had been involved in the organisation of that event, as well as being part of the May Queen Pageant for many years.

So, in their first year as being responsible for this traditional event, it was to prove one of those years when things went wrong. Sadly, during the week before the event Sheergar, the pony, died. There were multiple problems with the costumes which made them unusable and, to cap it all, the weather deteriorated. New costumes had to be made with only two weeks' notice and Helen and Heidi Pitt worked desperately to obtain material and make the dresses up before the day. Some, however were borrowed from the Laton Ash School of Dance.

In past years, the dancers were able to rehearse at their dance schools, and usually had full dress rehearsals. In the case of the Ambury School, there would be three or four rehearsals at the Sun Lounge (now Azur) at the Marina as well, before the event. Now there are two quick rehearsals at Blacklands School, where Helen teaches, on the Friday and Saturday before the event on Sunday

On the morning of the Pageant, the rain continued and a decision about the venue had to be made. So, at 11.00am, a hastily convened meeting decided that the event could not take place at the Castle and for the first time in 21 years the venue had to change. No alternatives had been prepared and it was just goodwill from Barbara Rogers, the manager of St Mary in the Castle that allowed the Pageant to take place. Numerous telephone calls were made to advise everybody of the situation and eventually everyone (almost) had been informed. Kevin Boorman and Barry Jones made a swift raid on the Castle and liberated the Maypole (to the detriment of Kevin's car).

Bethany Hill was a pupil of Pauline Ash of the Laton Ash School of dance. She went on to become the 2013 Hastings Carnival Queen.

Queen Bethany poses on the steps in St Mary's (mh)

The attendants rest on the stage (mh)

The entertainment was augmented by a French band called Les Derniere Trouvere. They are a folk band who play, and dress, in the medieval style and were in Hastings for the Jack-in-the-Green weekend. They were delighted to be asked to perform for the May Queen and gave the event a rousing finish. Even the Mad Jacks men Morris side turned up to help the afternoon.

Flower Girls and attendants take a bow (mh)

Les Derniere Trouvere

Mad Jack's Morris

2011

Queen Alice Quinnel-Fletcher

15 year old Alice Quinnel-Fletcher was crowned by the Mayor, Councillor Kim Forward at Hastings Castle

There was also another Queen present, Lynda Wodehouse from Dorking, who had successfully bid for the title of "Queen of Hastings Castle" for the Children in Need charity. This was an unexpected development for the organisers who felt that Lynda should have had an escort into the arena. The Mayor and Town Crier being already placed in the procession, another male with the suitable appearance was sought. Fortunately, one of the stalwarts of the Jack-in-the-Green weekend, Jon (Big Jon) Tigwell was dressed to kill in Tweed plus fours and agreed to be Queen Consort for the day. Nobody knows quite why Jon was dressed this way, and the great thing about this weekend is that nobody asked!

The Maypole dancers were beginning to be difficult to find. As the organiser in charge of the dancing, Helen Jones did not have the luxury of picking from a dance school, but relied on previous year's dancers and those who showed interest. At this time, due to the low profile of the event, there were not many who knew what the event was about and interest was low. However, it was decided to reduce the age limit to 10, and new, enthusiastic dancers were found.

Queen Alice with the new style Crown (ho)

The crowd of around 200 was entertained as usual by Hannah's Cat Morris, and "Les Derniere Trouveres", a French band in a medieval style of dress and music. They had come over again, having enjoyed the previous year in Hastings. Heather Leech agreed to be the MC and has filled that role ever since.

Hannah's Cat (ho)

The Garland competition took place after the crowning and Maypole dances.

The new style dresses (ho)

2012

Queen Sara Amini-Asil

Queen Sara (ho)

Deputy Mayor Alan Roberts crowned Sara Amini-Asil at the Castle on an overcast and windy day. This was to be the 22nd and final crowning at the Castle, although that was not known at the time.

Holly Sheldrake and The Fiddle Choir again provided the music, with Ian Dobson arranging the sound system.

Hannah's Cat Morris danced, and called on the younger members of the audience to join in with the Hooe Ribbon Dance.

Another new addition, the new Banner was unveiled this year. Designed and painted by Claire Fletcher, a local artist, it reflects the spirit of the Pageant.

The new Banner (u75)

The last procession at the Castle (ho)

2013

Queen Sophie Mepham

Twenty four years ago the May Queen Pageant was moved to the Castle to accommodate Council cost cutting, and as support to the Jack-in-the-Green weekend. This year the whole Country suffered cuts due to a recent recession and a weak economy, and Council budgets were cut even further. Consequently, Hastings Council was unable to cover the huge cost of building a temporary structure to enable access for the large crowds involved. This meant that the Castle was not prepared for an event.

The organisers therefore felt that this was a heaven sent opportunity to take the Pageant back to what could be called its spiritual home of Alexandra Park. So the Mayor Councillor Alan Roberts crowned Sophie Mepham on the Bandstand in the Park.

Where, previously, the Pageant took place on the Lower Lawn, this year the May Queen lead the procession from that starting point, through the Park. The horses and trap were surrounded by the Sweep, banner carrier, crown bearer (Andrew Prince, the grandson of the Chimney Sweep) and flower girls. The Maypole dancers and Hannah's Cat Morris followed.

After weeks of worry and guesswork, the organisers were overjoyed with the reaction of the public. Several dozen people followed the procession all the way to the Bandstand, and there were plenty of photographers both amateur and professional. On arrival the May Queen was greeted by the Town Crier and Mayor and a crowd which numbered almost one thousand. The crowning took place on the Bandstand after which, the dancers hailed the new Queen and danced the Maypole. Simon Costin, Director of the British Folk Museum, judged the Children's Garland Competition.

 Hannah's Cat performed their Morris, and then invited young and old to dance the Hooe Ribbon Dance.

To put the final gloss on the event, the day was sunny and warm, after months of cold weather, and the Park was a credit to the Parks and Gardens department who had worked hard to produce a wonderful environment.

The Procession through the Park (ic)

Queen Sophie (ho)

Ion Castro had been a Page Boy in 1958 and had returned to the Pageant as a photographer. We are grateful for his pictures which are some of the best of this event ever taken.

Ion had been a pupil of Miss Catt at the Orchard School of Speech and drama, and remembers, with affection, the double carriage driveway of Radcliffe House with the Pampas grass.

The scenes at the Bandstand (ic)

Catching up! (ho)

2014

Queen Ruby Webb

Another May Queen with a commendable track record. Ruby had been dancing the Maypole for a number of years. She was crowned by the Mayor, Councillor Alan Roberts on the Bandstand in Alexandra Park. When told she had been selected, Ruby appeared to be worried. When asked about this she said that she was worried that, having been May Queen, she would no longer be allowed to dance again! She was quickly reassured that she would be welcomed back next year.

After an extremely wet winter and early spring, it was a relief that the weather improved for the weekend of the May Bank holiday.

Queen Ruby with the bouquet from Hastings Council up! (mh)

For the last 3 years the crown had been commissioned as an individually handmade item by Angie Fox, and this year's offering can be seen in the following photograph. Flowers for the event were also donated by the local Sainsbury's. Staff from the "eat@ the Park" café led by the owners, Stephen and Louise Kelleher, set out the deck chairs and decorated the Bandstand with bunting. Hannah's Cat Morris completed the scene with flowers and ribbons.

It has always been an event which has been made possible by the good will of unpaid volunteers, and because of that it still has the atmosphere of a village fete with its rustic nature and simple charm.

Processing through the Park (ic/kp)

There was a similar programme to the previous year, but with the addition of a Punch and Judy show. London based Robert Styles gave two performances during the afternoon, and had the children (of all ages) enthralled.

As before, the procession set off from the lower lawn, and made their way through the Park to finish at the Bandstand.

During the research for this book, it was noted that the first Hastings May Queen, Rhona Powell wore a dress designed and made by the Hastings College of Art. When we approached the new Sussex Coast College in Hastings the head of the design department, Alison Hawkins, enthusiastically agreed to add a May Queen Dress to the curriculum. A competition was held, and the organisers had the unenviable task of judging the most suitable offering. The winner was Jess Wenden, whose dress was worn by Ruby.

Holly Sheldrake and the Fiddle Choir provided the music, and Hannah's Cat Ladies Morris side added to the fun. As well as the Morris dancing, the audience joined in with the Hooe Ribbon Dance.

Barry Jones was proud to have been the attending Sweep for the twentieth year, and Kevin Boorman represented the Council Tourism Dept. for the fifteenth time. Simon Costin again judged the Garland competition.

2014 at the Bandstand (kp)

Queen Ruby wearing the specially made crown

2015

Queen Bethan Jones

For the first time since the return to Alexandra Park, the weather had an impact on the event. After a dry April, the two days before the crowning were overcast, and rain started on the Saturday evening and carried on through the night. Sunday morning was the same and as midday approached decisions had to be made. Fortunately the rain stopped and the Pageant was possible. After some rearrangement of the programme, and with the determination of the participants, the event started an hour late. Richard Alan, a storyteller in the guise of an Elizabethan potato seller, held the first session inside the café. The Fiddle Choir then played on the Bandstand as the weather improved and as the audience started to grow. Eventually the audience numbered almost 400. This was down on previous years, but, given the weather conditions, a testament to the enhanced reputation of the event.

The Speech (ac)

The procession from the Lower Lawn started on time and was joined by the Town Crier, Jon Bartholomew. Jon had just returned from winning a major National Criers tournament and was resplendent in a new bespoke uniform.

So, after overcoming the weather, Queen Bethan arrived at the Bandstand to be crowned by the Mayor, Councillor Bruce Dowling. She was wearing a dress designed and made by Nicola Miller, a student of the Sussex Coast College, who had, again run the May Queen dress design as part of their curriculum. Nicola had been so determined to produce the dress to the highest standard that she had worked up to the last minute, and delivered the finished article at 9.15 the previous evening The crown had also been a last minute panic when it was realised the lady who had made the crown for the last few years was too unwell to make it. A local florist, "Fleur de Lynn" was approached, and a magnificent crown was produced.

Queen Bethan enthroned

The weather was not the only sadness this year. Beau, the horse who had pulled the cart for the May Queens of the last few years, had succumbed to an illness of the nervous system and died just a few days before the event.

As Beth is my daughter, she had attended the Hastings May Queen Pageant every year of her life, from being carried as a 4 month old baby, through to helping behind the

Queen Bethan with her proud parents

scenes and as a flower girl and eventually dancing for Irene Spillett. It was unfortunate that, having declined being May Queen last year in favour of Ruby Webb, that she experienced the disappointment of the bad weather, the lack of the horse drawn trap, and the fact that one of the dancers had not turned up through illness. This meant that she had to dance all the dances and not, as in previous Pageants, been seated to watch until dancing the last dance. However she thoroughly enjoyed the day and didn't stop smiling all afternoon.

On the Bandstand

Very little has been reported about the dancers over the years. I have watched the event for 20 years and have attended the practises for six, and I have found the utmost respect for these young ladies. In this year's Jack-in-the-Green finale on the West hill, a group of mature, experienced Morris dancers performed a Maypole set. They were trained by, and included Helen Jones and they performed well and were applauded loudly, but they were aware that it is not an easy thing to do. The May Queen dancers are aged between 9 and 15 and are accomplished in the dances. They are able to spot mistakes and rectify any misplaced plaiting. Helen has always made a point of allowing them to sort out the problems themselves and I am amazed by the skill that they have acquired.

It is always hard when one of these girls leaves, and this year we were sorry to say goodbye to Trudie Suggitt after 5 years as a dancer.

The 2015 Maypole Dancers

When the Pageants began, the dancers were taught to perform around the Maypole in a manner befitting the dance school ethos. The steps were rehearsed over many weeks, and the shapes of the dance were held to the highest standard. In many way the dances were a combination of folk dancing and ballet.

Nowadays the dances tend to be informal and the emphasis is on the fun element. Helen has now got a troupe of experienced dancers who are able to try a wider range of ribbon shapes, and the intention is to expand the number of dances. As the Pageant is no longer dance school centred, we are able to look at other features of the event in order to create an all-round entertainment. However, there is an imperative to continue the traditional elements, and even bring back some that would otherwise be lost.

Two traditions were revived this year. After more than 50 years the Pageant had a Robin Hood. The part was played by Andrew Prince. The second was in the speeches. At our request, the Mayor included the plea to the young to care for the flora and fauna of the town. This was started in 1946, when the Mayor crowned another Jones (Hazel).

It has now become a regular custom for the May Queen and some of her attendants to walk in the Monday morning Jack-in-the-Green procession. This picture shows Bethan (suitably face painted) holding the Pole for the adult Maypole dance on the stage.

✂ The Future ✂

There are no guarantees that Hastings will have a May Queen next year. It is only the enthusiasm of a few that keeps the tradition alive and it will not be missed by the majority of the population. Although there is strong backing from the local council's Tourism Department now, there is no certainty that interest couldn't wane, as it did in the 1980's. So, where is the hope?

The hope is in the youth. Helen and I do not expect to be organising the event for many more years, and we have to pass on the reins to somebody. We are satisfied that we know who could take it on and probably improve and enhance the ceremony. We also know that these people have the dedication that will guarantee the spirit is maintained, but the tradition must be valued by the people of Hastings to ensure its continuation.

We hope that you agree.

❧ Organisers/Producers
of the Hastings May Queen ❧

1934-74	Miss Dorothy Catt
1975-86	Miss Esme Child
1987-2009	Miss Irene Spillett
2010-15	Barry and Helen Jones

❧ Dance Directors for the
Hastings May Queen 1934 – 2015 ❧

1934-35	Mabel Wilis and Marjorie Kent
1936	Miss Joyce Tidman and Miss M. Coombes
1937-39	Miss Dorothy Purrock
1940-45	Miss Kathleen Neal
1946-66	Miss Phyllis Godfrey
1967-86	Miss Esme Child
1987-2009	Miss Irene Spillett
2010-	Mrs Helen Jones

(The honorific "Miss" is used for registered teachers of Dance.)

🕸 Hastings May Queens – Roll of Honour

1934 – 2015 🕸

1934	Rhona Powell	Warrior Square
1935	Margaret Hewett	Alexandra Park
1936	Peggy Ashman	Alexandra Park
1937	May Baker	Alexandra Park
1938	Peggy Nye	Alexandra Park
1939	Molly Parsons	Bal Edmund
1940	Norma Excell	St John's Vicarage
1941	Gwen Watford	St John's Vicarage
1942	Elizabeth Hayward	St John's Vicarage
1943	Lavender Seaward	St John's Vicarage
1944.	Mavis Stapley	St John's Vicarage
1945.	Joan Parks	Warrior Square
1946	Hazel Jones	Warrior square
1947	Claudine Burton	Warrior Square
1948	Ann Hills	Linton Gardens
1949	Valerie Hurcombe	Linton Gardens
1950	Shirley Waller	Linton Gardens
1951	Patricia Walsh	Linton Gardens
1952	Mary Dutton	Warrior Square
1953	Anne Veness	Alexandra Park
1954	Petrina Cornwell	Alexandra Park
1955	Angela Burton	Alexandra Park
1956	Sylvia Dale	Alexandra Park
1957	Beverley Cornwell	Alexandra Park
1958	Susan Hyne	Alexandra Park
1959	Jennifer Betteridge	Alexandra Park
1960	Deidre Wyatt	Alexandra Park
1961	Margaret White	Alexandra Park
1962	Jane Hills	White Rock
1963	Petula Portell	Alexandra Park
1964	Rosemary Binge	White Rock
1965	Linda Glazier	White Rock
1966	Yvonne Catt	Alexandra Park
1967	Jane Burrows	Alexandra Park

1968	Alison Hoare	Alexandra Park
1969	Jeannette Vidler	Alexandra Park
1970	Gail Benet	White Rock
1971	Deborah Burden	Alexandra Park
1972	Angela Wren	White Rock
1973	Judith Anne Cresswell	Alexandra Park
1974	Carolyn Nash	Alexandra Park
1975	Heather Alexander	Alexandra Park
1976	Elaine Waller	Alexandra Park
1977	Henrietta Hammet	Alexandra Park
1978	Janet West	White Rock
1979	Caroline Bruce	White Rock
1980	Teresa Woodhouse	Alexandra Park
1981	Amanda Rapp	White Rock
1982	Samantha Rapp	Alexandra Park
1983	Wendy Thornton	Alexandra Park
1984	Wendy Thornton	Alexandra Park
1985	Emma Coulman	Falaise Hall
1986	Emma Stace	White Rock
1987	Nicola Rodmell	Alexandra Park
1988	Lisa Walters	Alexandra Park
1989	Heidi Welsh	Alexandra Park
1990	Claire Hills	Hastings Castle
1991	Debbie Martin	Hastings Castle
1992	Natalie Driver	Hastings Castle
1993	Charlotte Lord	Hastings Castle
1994	Emma Hardy	Hastings Castle
1995	Anna-Leigh Glover	Hastings Castle
1996		Hastings Castle
1997	Gemma Dadswell	Hastings Castle
1998	Katie Chenery	Hastings Castle
1999	Elizabeth Salt	Hastings Castle
2000	Eugenie Demeza	Hastings Castle
2001	Abigail Shillabeer	Hastings Castle
2002	Siobhan Steuart-Pownell	Hastings Castle
2003	Nicola Martin	Hastings Castle
2004	Kirsty Whittington	Hastings Castle
2005	Anna-Marie Kimber	Hastings Castle

2006	Alison Frencer	Hastings Castle
2007	Ashley Rudd	Hastings Castle
2008	Michaela Botting	Hastings Castle
2009	Victoria Coleman	Hastings Castle
2010	Bethany Hill	St Mary in the Castle
2011	Alice Quinnel-Fletcher	Hastings Castle
2012	Sarah Amini-Asil	Hastings Castle
2013	Sophie Mepham	Alexandra Park
2014	Ruby Webb	Alexandra Park
2015	Bethan Jones	Alexandra Park

❧ Bibliography ❧

Brand's Antiquities (John Brand) Vol. 1 Cambridge Library Collection University Press 1813/2011 ISBN 978-1-108-03646-7

Whitelands College May Queen Festival (Malcolm Coe) Whitelands College 1981 The Hastings traditional Jack-in-the-Green (Keith Leech) Hastings Borough Council 2008   ISBN 978-0-901536-10-5

A Sussex Garland (Tony Wales) Countryside Books 1986/7 ISBN 0-905392-64-7

Spring and Summer Customs in Sussex, Kent and Surrey (Fran and Geoff Doel and Tony Deane) Meresborough Books 1995 ISBN 0948193-832

The Folklore of Sussex (Jacqueline Simpson) BT Batsford Ltd 1973 ISBN 0-7134-0240-7

❧ Acknowledgements ❧

Photographs

apm = Andre Palfrey-Martin
as = Anne Slacke
ba = Brian Lawes
cb = Caroline Aitkin (nee Bruce)
ho = Hastings and St Leonards Observer
ic = Ion Castro
jh = June Hills
Mc = Miss Catt collection
mh = Mark Harrison - Aramanth photography
pa = Pauline Ash
rc = Ruth Carter and the Westfield History Society
tl = Tom Lawrence
u75 = Urban 75 (via Flickr)
wt = Wendy Thornton
kp = Kellee Pepper

❧ With grateful thanks to ❧

Anne Slacke for her memories, and the help in finding Miss Catt's collection.
Betty Scarbro (Nee Tingle) for photos and memories of the beginning.
Brian Lawes for the" Hastings Pictorial" research.

❧ About the Authors ❧

Barry has been a Chimney Sweep in Hastings for the last 23 years. He has been actively involved with the Hastings Traditional Jack-in-the-Green festival for 20 years, including the attending of the May Queen.

Born in 1953 above his Grandfather's High Street bakers shop, he lived in the Old Town of Hastings until 1962. Having lived in Hastings and St Leonards all his life he has a particular awareness of the history of the area since the war years, and of the local "quirks" and traditions.

Helen has lived in Hastings most of her life, and has taught at Blacklands, a local primary school for over 20 years. Her father was a vicar who was the incumbent of a long-demolished church in Priory Road. She grew up with a close involvement with the Parish, and, through her teaching, has maintained contacts with local people through more than one generation.